Mixed Ability Teaching

Problems and Possibilities

Margaret I. Reid,
Louise R. Clunies-Ross,
Brian Goacher and Carol Vile

The NFER-Nelson Publishing Company Ltd

Published by The NFER-Nelson Publishing Company Ltd.,
Darville House, 2 Oxford Road East,
Windsor, Berks. SL4 1DF.

First Published 1981
© NFER, 1981
ISBN 0-85633-2321
Code 8083 021

Distributed in the USA by Humanities Press Inc.,
Atlantic Highlands, New Jersey 07716 USA

Photoset by Vantage Photosetting Co. Ltd.
Printed in Great Britain by
Biddles Ltd., Guildford, Surrey

Contents

Chapter VII: Pointers

2685 .

List of Tables

List of Figures

Foreword

Those who enjoy the excitement of the barricade may well be disappointed by the treatment accorded in this report to what has become a highly emotive issue. There is little comfort to be derived from its content either by those who maintain that mixed ability grouping *per se* affords a short-cut to the millennium or by those of their opponents who identify it as a major threat to the maintenance of educational standards.

The preliminary sections of the report serve to lower the temperature of this debate and to raise the level of discourse for any future discussion of the issues involved.

The authors argue cogently that what has been commonly overlooked during the course of this controversy is that all groups of pupils or students, however they may be selected or constituted, are to some degree mixed with regard to ability (however this attribute might be defined) – and, indeed, with regard to many other characteristics that are manifestly related to the educational progress of their members. Wherever two or three are gathered together individual differences will become apparent. A school's organizational arrangements, whether these involve streaming, setting or the conscious pursuit of 'planned heterogeneity', can affect only the range of ability within the groups that are formed.

Furthermore it can be demonstrated that deliberate attempts to maximize or to minimize the range of ability within any group are commonly frustrated by factors over which teachers have little or no control. A school's catchment area, for example, may yield an intake of pupils from which it is not possible to compose groups that manifest as wide a range of ability as that which is characteristic of the population as a whole. Nor is it possible to measure 'ability' – or any other attribute chosen as the criterion for the purposes of grouping – with a degree of accuracy sufficient to ensure that the desired degree of similarity or variety is achieved.

If we accept that mixed ability grouping is, to some extent, an inevitable outcome of any procedure for assigning pupils to separate bands, streams, classes or sets, the central issue on which this report is focussed is clearly relevant to the concerns not only of those who are committed to mixed ability grouping as the preferred form of school organization but to those of all who have an interest in the teaching and learning process. This central issue, which is reflected in the title of the report, is mixed ability *teaching*. Mixed ability teaching involves the attempt so to fashion or adapt teaching methods and approaches as to make due allowance for the individual needs and capabilities of every pupil. The substance of the report is based on the views and experiences of a large and varied sample of heads and teachers who have undertaken this formidable task. It provides documented evidence, of the only kind available to us, concerning the perceived advantages and shortcomings of attempts, in a variety of circumstances and in relation to a wide range of disciplines and activities, to match modes of instruction to the needs of individual pupils. It illustrates the kinds of constraint that can hinder the enterprise: the shortcomings of current programmes of pre-service and in-service training; over-large classes; the lack of equipment, resources, facilities, storage space and adequate ancillary help. It also furnishes examples of ingenuity and application in overcoming these disabilities. The outcome, as one would expect, is not a clear-cut verdict in favour of or against the approaches that are exemplified in the case-studies contained in the report. What emerges is a sizeable array of topics for discussion which are stimulating enough to engage the attention of all teachers who recognize the possibility that current teaching practices are susceptible of improvement.

Alfred Yates
9 February 1981

Acknowledgements

Research is a corporate activity and throughout the project we received encouragement, advice and assistance from many sources. Sadly, we are unable to name those to whom perhaps we owe most – the heads and teachers who gave in many cases hours of their time to exploring issues associated with mixed ability teaching with us. We have quoted from them extensively and in many parts this report is theirs.

The research was guided in its various stages by a Steering Committee and to its members – Mr. E. G. Beynon, Dr. C. Burstall, Mr. J. Caulfield, Miss J. Chreseson, HMI, Mr. G. Lee, Professor W. D. Wall, Dr. R. W. West, Miss S. D. Wood and Mr. A. Yates (Chairman) – we give our thanks for their counsel and sustained interest in the project over a number of years. We would like also to record our debt to colleagues who have given us their time and expertise and we thank especially Mrs. L. Kendall for her guidance with the statistical analyses, Miss J. May for providing excellent library support and Dr. J. Bradley and Mr. D. Foxman for reading the manuscript and making many helpful suggestions.

It is apparent from the authorship of this book that the research was the work of a team and clear-cut attributions are difficult to make. Chapters One, Three, Four and Seven are mainly the work of the senior author. Brian Goacher was responsible for the reporting of teachers' perceptions of the advantages and disadvantages of mixed ability grouping in Chapter Five, Louise Clunies-Ross provided the subject by subject analysis in Chapter Six, whilst Carol Vile contributed the description of the sample in Chapter Two. The typing of the report's final draft was most ably undertaken by Mrs. A. Symmonds assisted by Mrs. S. Box and Mrs. H. Warren.

Margaret I. Reid
January 1981

Chapter One

The Project: Its Aims and Scope

'The Working Party found that in a very small number of the schools visited, pupils were working at an appropriate level and pace in mixed ability groups in all the subjects and year groups to which this organization applied. In others there were examples of excellent work in particular subject areas. Nevertheless, in most of the schools visited HM Inspectors felt concern about the level, pace and scope of the work in a significant number of subjects. This concern was sometimes on behalf of pupils throughout the ability range; more frequently it related to the extremes of the range; and most frequently it related to the work of the most able pupils' (DES, 1978).

'Erosion of teacher authority and use of mixed ability teaching were identified yesterday by the National Association of School-masters – Union of Women Teachers as two major factors militating against higher education standards' (*Guardian*, 15.3.77).

'. . . increased social mixing associated with heterogeneous ability groups in years one and two has been demonstrated, and so have the generally comparable academic standards in the two systems of ability grouping. There are academic differences, particularly some advantages for less able children in mixed ability forms, but these do not mask the overall similarities of the results from the two grouping systems . . .' (Newbold, 1977).

'Mixed ability teaching is the next logical step to take on the road to comprehensive education and it promises to give teachers an opportunity to lift the secondary curriculum out of the nineteenth century. Parents should be asking, "Why is my child not receiving

1

mixed ability teaching?"' (M. B. Doran, *Guardian*, 5.9.78).

'The retention of mixed ability grouping up to the end of year 2 or 3 for all or the great majority of subjects is not uncommon in ILEA schools and is most often accompanied by a continuation of undifferentiated teaching; this frequently occurs at a level barely suitable for the middle of the ability range in the group, leaving the least able unheeded and the most able unchallenged' (DES, 1980).

Two issues, closely interrelated, have been foremost in discussions on secondary education in the past three decades. The first has concerned whether pupils of widely varying abilities should be educated together under one roof and the second whether they can effectively be taught alongside each other in the same class. Mixed ability teaching, as it is commonly called, has acquired, as the above quotations demonstrate, a body of protagonists and opponents, with claims and counter-claims emanating in profusion from various sections of the education service and indeed from outside it. The research reported in the chapters which follow sought to explore such claims and counter-claims with those who are arguably in the best position of all to comment – the heads and teachers in schools which employ this mode of organization for teaching purposes.

1.   The meaning of mixed ability

It is not uncommon in any argument for those taking part to spend a great deal of time only to find that they were all along talking about different things. One of the functions of research in education is to clarify areas of controversy, to draw attention to the multiplicity of meanings attached to phrases and labels which through excessive exposure have become so familiar that it is assumed that all who use them share a common interpretation. Thus the DES-sponsored research on comprehensive education carried out by the Foundation from 1965–71 demonstrated the immense diversity of those schools labelled as 'comprehensive' – a diversity which rendered much of the generalized debate on these institutions meaningless. Discussion of mixed ability teaching faces similar if not greater problems.

Consensus on what constitutes ability has consistently eluded social scientists and educationists. Because of this, one of the first stumbling blocks in discussing mixed ability teaching concerns what precisely it is that is being mixed. This dilemma is sooner or later revealed in much of the writing on the topic. If, for example, we look at the opening paragraph of the report of an ILEA inspectorate survey (1976) on mixed ability grouping, we read that 'In 1971 the Inspectorate published for Inner London secondary schools an inspectorate paper making suggestions to schools considering the introduction of mixed *ability* teaching. Since then, there has been a considerable increase in the number of schools organizing their teaching in mixed *attainment* groups for at least part of the secondary courses. It therefore seemed an appropriate time to have constructive discussions with teachers about problems of the management of mixed *ability* classes.' The report goes on to define mixed *ability* grouping: 'in its purest form this type of organization groups pupils in such a way that each class in the year group is assumed to have an equal *range of attainment.* Each class remains together for all subjects, except where separately grouped by sex (as in physical education) or divided into sub-groups (as in craft work).' The description assumes a situation where attainment remains constant across subjects – or is it really a general ability factor that is being referred to? The confusion begs resolution; the relationship between ability and attainment is one which has bedevilled psychometricians from the outset. Important factors determining that relationship may be motivation, attitudes, specific skills, and as one writer points out, some teachers confuse 'mixed ability' with mixed skills, mixed attitudes, mixed motivation and mixed attainment (Scott, 1976). Adelman (1976) makes a similar point when he asks 'By what criteria, tests and reports is a mixed ability class constituted? There is no consistency of selection across secondary schools. I suspect that generally pupils are selected not by their ability but on their school achievements; on the basis of success by the criteria and standards of the school rather than a standard psychometric test of intellectual potential. "Ability" may be assessed by psychometric tests. Achievement is bound up with the social context of teaching and learning. The docile and obedient – the rule-following are mixed with a population of "hard cases" – a "mixed ability" bunch of resistors to the social order of the school.'

Adelman's suspicions of how pupils are selected for mixed ability classes are confirmed by the practices of allocating pupils to groups described in Chapter Four. Mixed 'ability' groups may be formed on the basis of pupils' scores on psychometric tests (i.e. *ability*) but frequently these are supplemented or supplanted by primary teachers' assessments (adding factors concerned with *achievement, motivation* and *attitudes*), by performance on reading tests (*skills*) or groups may simply be formed by random sampling, alphabetical ordering, or on a friendship/neighbourhood basis.

The end-product will of course always be a mixed ability group in the sense that all groups – even the most rigorously streamed – contain a range of ability and also a range of attainments. It is, then, the width of the range which is the central issue; when teachers use the phrase 'mixed ability grouping', as applying to their classes, what is implied is that these groups contain a wider range of whatever is meant by ability than would have been the case had some form of selective grouping been applied. The actual ability and attainment mix in their classes, however, will vary, first according to the composition of the school's catchment and second according to the criteria and procedures employed to allocate children to classes. The immense variety of intake of schools labelled as comprehensive was well-documented in the first NFER survey of comprehensive education (Monks, 1968); in the nine schools studied by the ILEA inspectorate (ILEA 1976), numbers of group 1 ('above average') children per double-class of 60 pupils entering the schools varied from 4 to 12 and group 3 children ('below average') from 13 to 25. The variety in allocation procedures has already been mentioned, and it should be pointed out here that it is not simply the *range* of abilities which determines the mix in a class but the nature of their distribution.

Hence, just as there is wide divergence as to *what* is being mixed, so there is great variation in the mixing process itself. There is no agreement, in short, as to what is meant by 'ability' and similarly no consensus on the 'mixing'. Because of this, many have sought alternative terminologies. 'Heterogeneous' ability groups may be contrasted with 'homogeneous' groupings; but these terms too beg definition, for any group of children may be described as heterogeneous in the same way as any group may be called mixed, and again the essential differences lie in the range and distribution of abilities. Perhaps more common is the use of the terms 'un-streaming' and 'non-streaming'. Streaming has been defined as 'the division of pupils into classes in which the average general attainment of pupils in a class is assumed to be higher than that in the class next below it in the list. The composition of each class is then kept the same for most subjects' (ILEA, 1976). Unstreaming, by contrast, according to one writer, describes the situation where 'a year group corresponding to a normal distribution of ability (excluding ESN and SSN pupils) is subdivided into smaller groups, each reflecting the range of ability in the year group' (Scott, 1976). But, as already pointed out, schools vary in their catchment, and many do not receive a normal distribution of ability; classes described as 'unstreamed' may therefore differ profoundly because of this. Non-streaming may in practice mean grouping other than by abilities (friendship and neighbourhood groups, alphabetical groupings, etc.) and the groups formed in these ways are sometimes described as 'natural' or 'unselected' groups. The nature of the mix of abilities, attainments, skills and motivations is left to chance, the assumption being that some kind of randomness will ensure groups which are roughly comparable. It is, however, very common in such situations, and indeed in those where an attempt is made to contrive comparable ability and attainment distributions among classes, for teachers to report that there are always one or two forms in any year group which 'stand out'.

The term 'mixed ability' grouping is frequently used synonymously with heterogeneous, unstreamed, non-streamed, natural or unselected groups. It is a popular umbrella term covering a wide variety of organizations and procedures in very different school environments. Hence when the project was first publicized, and schools who wished to take part were invited to supply details of the form and extent of mixed ability grouping in their schools, we received responses from grammar and secondary modern schools as well as from schools designated as comprehensive. Schools identified themselves as having mixed ability groups if they employed unstreamed groups within broad bands of ability, or if they used unstreamed groups for all but the slowest, or sometimes brightest children. The term was also perceived as covering the situation where unstreamed groups were used for those parts of the curriculum sometimes described as 'non-academic' (physical education, art, religious education, woodwork, home economics, etc.) but selective groups were employed for subjects such as mathematics, languages and science. It is important to remember in the context of the debate on mixed ability teaching that statements may derive from experiences in any of these very different situations.

The title of the project indicates its concern with mixed ability *teaching*. Elliot (1976) draws a distinction between 'teaching in mixed ability groups' and 'mixed ability teaching'. 'Mixed ability teaching', he writes, 'implies a certain kind of teaching, whereas any kind of teaching can go on in mixed ability groups.' Together with Bailey (1976) he believes that this kind of teaching 'focuses on individuals rather than on class or group'. The teaching model 'teacher to whole class' can only be appropriate where individual differences are at a minimum. Bailey elaborates the point: 'What I mean by mixed ability teaching is any form of teaching which involves the teacher working with individuals rather than groups. This kind of teaching can, of course, go on whether the group is allegedly homogeneous or not. The teacher simply recognizes all groups as mixed ability groups, which indeed they are. Any form of teaching is mixed ability teaching, then, that dispenses with the idea that groups of children can learn things at the same time and at the same rate and pass on to other things at the same time as one another.' He goes on to present a cogent argument that if mixed ability teaching is harmful, it is harmful in precisely those areas where children need to work together in groups. Bridges (1976) however presents a contrary viewpoint. Whilst noting the variety of classroom organization which falls under the banner of mixed ability teaching, he stresses that for some people 'mixed ability teaching is virtually synonymous with group work, and its virtue lies especially in the experience it gives of co-operative group endeavour' – a view supported by E. M. Hoyles formerly of Vauxhall Manor school: 'One of the main features of mixed ability classroom organization is the numerous occasions in which children need to work in groups.' The variety of modes of classroom organization in different areas of the curriculum is explored in Chapter Six.

As to the meaning of each of the three component words of the project's title there is, then, a wide diversity of views – a diversity which reflects itself in the aims, organizations, procedures and methods employed in those schools claiming to employ 'mixed ability teaching'. This report sets out to document that diversity. The words it uses are to a very large extent the words of the teachers who have taken part in the project, and as such mirror a collective wealth of experience in what is still regarded as an innovation in school and classroom organization. In order to report that diversity, it was important that the project did not set out with a fixed idea of what it understood by mixed ability teaching; on the other hand, some working definition of the area of enquiry was essential if teachers were to know what they were being asked about. A mixed ability class was therefore defined as '*a teaching unit which is not streamed, banded or setted and which is in a non-selective school. The class may or may not contain pupils from a remedial department*'.

2. The problems of comparison

Such classes were common in the mid-seventies for pupils in their early years of secondary education. An NFER survey carried out in 1974–75 of over a thousand comprehensive schools found that just over half employed mixed ability groups as the mode of organization for most of the curriculum in the first year, 37 per cent continued into the second year and 25 per cent into the third. Throughout, however, fairly extensive use was made of setting for such subjects as mathematics and modern languages. Hence of those schools with a predominantly mixed ability organization in the first year, 46 per cent employed setting for some subjects; in the second year this rose to 77 per cent and in the third year, of the quarter of schools still persisting with heterogeneous groups for most of the curriculum, 91 per cent nevertheless used setting for some subjects.

The survey produced a rich volume of comment from head teachers concerning mixed ability teaching; it was variously seen as a gimmick and a godsend and there were many pleas for a research which would elucidate some of the issues associated with it. A year previously, the Assistant Masters Association, reporting on a survey it had undertaken in 1972, had also underlined the need for research to 'evaluate the implications and consequences before more schools introduce this method of grouping' (AMA, 1974). Many of the requests for research reflected the desire for a comparative study; indeed this remained one of the most common pleas received by the project throughout its life. There is little doubt that for many, any major research into mixed ability teaching should have at its heart the question 'Do children learn as well as they would if they were taught in classes containing a narrower range of ability?' (i.e. classes which are streamed, setted or banded). Like many of the apparently 'key' questions in education (comprehensive versus selective schools, open versus closed classrooms) it presents the researcher with a daunting task, because beneath its apparently simple formulation there lie many more questions, the answers to which are dependent on people's objectives in education and society and the criteria by which they assess whether such objectives have been achieved. The technical difficulties in answering comparative questions of this kind are well-known; essentially the problem is one of disentangling from an almost endless list of variables – home, school, teacher and classroom – what is relevant to a child's learning. It is not, therefore, surprising, in view of such complexity, that studies so far carried out which have sought to make direct comparison of streamed and unstreamed groups have been inconclusive in their findings – a fact too readily glossed over by some proponents of mixed ability teaching. Thus one writer (Davies, 1975), concluding his introductory review of the literature, claims that 'the act of faith which led many teachers to turn to mixed ability grouping in the first place has received more and more support, on the evidence of both experience and a growing body of research. From this point in the book I shall assume that the case in favour of abandoning streaming is made and concentrate on the practical implications of this at the school level.'

A more balanced presentation of the evidence appears in a helpful review by Morrison (1976), who concludes that 'the only general agreement about the results of research hitherto is that no agreement has resulted', a view supported among others by Yates (1966), who describes the evidence as 'plentiful but conflicting'; by Passow (1966) – 'the quantity of research is great, the quality irregular and the results generally inconclusive'; by Borg (1964) – 'the most tenable conclusion is that neither ability grouping nor random grouping has a consistent general effect on achievement at any of the levels tested'; and by Ross *et al.* (1972) – 'many pieces of evidence are available in the streaming and non-streaming argument but the findings of different research are often diametrically opposed to one another or inconclusive'.

Passow, seeking to account for this inconclusiveness, cites the following reasons: (1) the variety of aims and purposes, (2) too small samples, (3) the varying durations of the studies, (4) inadequate selection of samples and controls, (5) the failure to take account of teaching content and method, (6) the tendency to ignore the teacher factor, (7) the general failure to evaluate changes in the personal-social behaviour of pupils, and (8) the absence of any examination of the effects of grouping practice on teachers and administrators. Of these, perhaps the first is most critical, being beset by the problems of definition discussed at the beginning of this chapter and also by the nature of the outcome expected or required of the research. For, as Yates (1966) points out, 'one of the reasons why research has not served to settle or even diminish the controversies that centre around some grouping practices is because the differences of view involved are not entirely or even mainly about the measurable educational consequences of these practices. The sharpest conflicts would seem to be about the more far-reaching influences that grouping procedures – interschool groupings particularly – can exert on the structure of society as a whole, and on the distribution within it of privileges and opportunities.' Also crucial, is Passow's point concerning the failure of studies to take account of teaching content and method; the measurement of product has not been accompanied by the study of process. This is demonstrated in two British studies which preceded the present research. Barker Lunn's (1970) study of children in streamed and unstreamed primary schools and Newbold's (1975) research at Banbury School in Oxfordshire concur in the general tenor of their findings: few significant differences on academic measures and more favourable attitudes to school and peers from average and less able children in unstreamed classes. But these results were far from clear cut. Newbold found that differences between one streamed class and another and between one unstreamed class and another were generally greater than differences between the streamed and the unstreamed groups. The validity of Barker Lunn's approach, where the emphasis was also on measurement of product, may be questioned by the fact that when she went into supposedly unstreamed classes, she found children separated into groups according to their ability and quite as apart as if walls divided them.

These, and other studies, provided the clue for our approach. It seemed that any further investigation of mixed ability teaching must take account of the classroom process and relate assessment of outcomes – insofar as this is possible – to what actually happens in the classroom. Hence the project described in the pages which follow started from the point that many schools employed mixed ability groups, in the early years of secondary education at least, and was concerned with looking at its functioning in the classroom. For even if the record of the comparative studies were ignored and resources were available to carry out the extensive feasibility studies and methodological explorations which would be essential if past mistakes were to be avoided, it is doubtful whether the findings would be heeded by those committed to one or other side of the debate. As one teacher said to us: 'We shall still continue with mixed ability, despite your findings (he mistakenly thought the project was comparative) because that is the system we believe in.' Those in the 'middle ground', the uncommitted and the questioning, are likely to be more interested in, and helped by, an analysis and discussion of those issues associated with the teaching of mixed ability groups which teachers have encountered in the course of their experience.

3.   The nature of the enquiry

The research, which started in October 1975 and extended until December 1978 was designed in two stages. In stage one we tried through discussion with nearly 500 heads and teachers to map out what appeared to be the major issues. Its focus was on teachers' perceptions of the benefits, disadvantages and difficulties for their pupils and for themselves which seemed to be associated with mixed ability grouping. We were concerned with why and how schools had adopted this mode of organization, the changes they had found necessary in their ways of working and the strategies, materials and techniques employed by teachers of different subjects to meet the needs of groups of children varying widely in their abilities. Certain areas of concern emerged as being of particular importance to teachers in schools – such as the organization and preparation required for mixed ability teaching, resources and teaching approaches in the classroom, catering for the needs of the most and least able pupils – and these provided an agenda of areas of enquiry for the second phase of the project, which took the form of intensive studies in selected schools. It should be emphasized that the project was in no sense comparative; instead it sought to evaluate mixed ability teaching in the light of its apparent pay-offs, the problems encountered and the degree to which such problems could be resolved.

This present report gives the findings from the project's first 'mapping out' stage, in which 29 schools in five areas of the country took part. All were comprehensive schools, selected to provide a variety of catchment factors and with differing lengths of experience of mixed ability teaching. A further criterion for selecting the schools in each area was that they should be situated near enough to each other to make inter-school group discussions of selected themes feasible. Area one was rural, with schools located in country towns, some with light industry, and serving the neighbouring farming communities. The schools had introduced mixed ability grouping for first-year pupils when they received their first comprehensive intake in 1972 (in the case of four schools) or 1973 (one school). Sizes ranged from 567 pupils to 1,155 and all five schools were mixed. The schools in areas two and three, by contrast, were mostly large city schools; only one had fewer than 1,000 pupils and six of the 12 schools had over 1,500. Lengths of experience of mixed ability teaching varied, but several schools were among the pioneers of this form of grouping, having introduced it in the mid-60s. Area three contained the only two single-sex schools in the study – one a boys' school and one a girls'. The six schools in area four drew their pupils from the surrounding rural mining communities, and all were fairly large, with sizes ranging from just over 1,000 pupils to 1,800. The earliest introduction of mixed ability grouping was in 1967, the latest in 1975, concurrent with comprehensive reorganization. Schools in area five were located in or near an overspill development town and again demonstrated a variety of lengths of experience of unstreamed grouping – from one to nine years – and ranged in size from 410 to 940 pupils.

4. Gathering the data

A common procedure for gathering information was followed in all schools. First, basic information on the year groups and subjects where mixed ability grouping was employed, together with details of size, staffing and remedial arrangements, was sought. On the basis of this information, the team selected approximately one-quarter of each school's staff, representative of different subjects and levels of appointment, to discuss with them in interview, issues related to mixed ability teaching. Prior to the interview, staff completed a questionnaire on the subjects they taught to mixed ability and non-mixed ability classes in each year, the length and nature of their teaching experience, their total teaching load, the time spent with mixed ability classes and their professional training, both pre- and in-service. The interview was used to explore with teachers the extent to which they considered their subjects to lend themselves to a mixed ability approach, the advantages and disadvantages they perceived this mode of organization to have for pupil and teacher and the methods they used for organizing learning within their classroom. Teachers were asked to describe any particular difficulties they had encountered, together with approaches found useful in meeting these. The sample included teachers who were not currently teaching any unstreamed classes, and their views on mixed ability teaching were also elicited; they were further asked to comment on the advantages and disadvantages of selective grouping. Heads of department were in addition asked questions concerning the organization and operation of mixed ability teaching in their departments. Details of the sampling procedures adopted for the selection of teachers for interview are given in Chapter Two.

Finally, the heads of schools were interviewed to discuss broader issues of policy and institutional organization. The reasons for the adoption of unstreamed groupings were discussed, as well as the mode of their introduction. Much of the interview was focused on arrangements for the administration of mixed ability teaching – timetabling, length of teaching period, provision of resources – and its implications for the curriculum, departmental or faculty organization and the deployment of the school plant. Heads were also invited to comment on their policy concerning the recruitment of staff for mixed ability teaching, the teaching difficulties which staff had brought to their notice arising from it and any provision, past or current, for the in-service education of staff either in or outside their schools. Procedures for allocating children to groups were explored, together with the school's policy towards arranging the learning of the less able.

5.   The report

The programme described above generated a wealth of data; as is very apparent, there is no 'party line' among those teachers practising unstreamed teaching, and the many facets of this extremely complex subject are well-represented in the pages which follow. The next chapter describes the sample of teachers whose evidence forms the bulk of this report, whilst Chapter Three explores the reasons which led schools to opt for mixed ability grouping and the procedures employed for its introduction and organization. Chapter Four examines how schools allocated pupils to teaching groups and Chapter Five presents an analysis of teachers' perceptions of the advantages and disadvantages of mixed ability teaching in practice. Difficulties in teaching unstreamed groups are frequently associated with the nature of particular subjects, and Chapter Six focuses on the degree to which teachers in different disciplines perceived their subjects as suitable for teaching to unstreamed groups, and the methods they employed in their classrooms. The report concludes by reviewing those factors which the evidence of the enquiry suggests as critical for the effective implementation of mixed ability teaching.

Chapter Two

The Sample of Teachers

The twenty-nine schools selected for the first stage of the project had the common characteristic of being comprehensive schools with experience of mixed ability grouping for all or part of the curriculum in the early years of secondary education at least. They provided a sample of schools in which most of the staff taught some mixed ability groups and where interest in questions concerning various approaches to grouping pupils was apparent by the very fact of their participation in the project. From the researchers' point of view they furnished the opportunity of studying mixed ability teaching in terms of school organization and classroom practice in a variety of contexts.

In order to select staff for interview, the teachers in each school were considered as two populations: heads of department and other staff (excluding the head). The sampling procedure sought to ensure that all subjects were adequately represented and that certain key areas were included in every school: these were English, mathematics, modern languages and science. Accordingly, the heads of these departments were interviewed in each school, together with a one-in-five sample of the remaining heads of department. A similar sample (i.e. 20 per cent) was taken from the population of staff other than heads of department. The sample in the case of each school was checked to make sure that it was representative of the total population of teachers in terms of (a) the proportions of staff teaching mixed ability classes as compared with those teaching only selective groups; (b) the proportion of probationers and (c) the proportion of part-time staff. Because of the selective sampling of heads of department the curriculum areas of English, mathematics, modern languages and science had considerably greater representation than other subjects.

14

1. Some characteristics of the sample

The original sample comprised 496 teachers, but owing to varied circumstances such as difficulties with timetabling, sickness, etc., the team was unable to interview 17 of these. The final population of 479 teachers interviewed represented 97 per cent of the original sample. Four hundred and three teachers were identified as being substantially involved in teaching mixed ability classes, 24 as being involved almost exclusively with non-mixed ability groups and 52 as teaching selective groups only.

Overall, men outnumbered women in the sample by nearly 5:3. The ratio of men to women in the total population of maintained secondary school teachers at the time of the enquiry was roughly 5:4 and whilst this ratio was approximated in three of our five areas, in the remaining two – areas one and four – men outnumbered women by 9:3 and 7:3 respectively. One hundred and sixty nine of the teachers interviewed were heads of departments and only 17 per cent of these were women. The sample of teachers included some on each of the Burnham salary scales one to five (senior teachers being classified as scale 5) but differed significantly from the total population of teachers mainly due to the fact that the highest scale point (scale 5) was underrepresented.

Among the factors likely to influence teachers' perceptions of various grouping practices are the length and nature of their previous teaching experience. For the purposes of this investigation teachers were grouped into four categories of service (a) under one year's experience (b) one to five years' experience (c) six to ten years' (d) over ten years'. The proportion of teachers from the sample in each category is shown by area in Figure 2.1A. Probationer teachers formed 10 per cent of the total sample, whilst the other three categories were well represented, comprising 33 per cent, 23 per cent and 34 per cent of the sample respectively. Of the 169 heads of departments in the sample 65 per cent had over ten years' experience, whilst at the other end of the scale 11 per cent had between one and five years' experience. Interesting and statistically significant differences were found between teachers in different areas. In area one the proportion of teachers with lengthy experience was considerably higher than in other areas, and the proportion of those with relatively few years' service considerably lower. Fifty-seven per cent of staff interviewed in area one had over ten years' experience, a further 15 per cent had between one and five years service and six per cent were probationers. A markedly different pattern emerged in areas 3 and 4 where the interview population comprised a comparatively large proportion of relatively inexperienced teachers, and a smaller proportion of staff with over ten years' service. In area four, for example, the latter made up 28 per cent of the interviewees, whilst 35 per cent had one to five years' experience, and 12 per cent were probationers. Comparable figures for area 3 were 32 per cent, 40 per cent and nine per cent respectively. The remaining two areas (areas 2 and 5) followed the pattern reported for the total sample.

Just over one-fifth of the teachers interviewed had no experience other than that gained in their present comprehensive schools, in addition to the 10 per cent who were probationers. Nearly 10 per cent of teachers had previous experience in other comprehensive schools, and seven and three per cent respectively in secondary modern schools and in grammar schools only. By far the largest group, however, accounting for some 40 per cent of the sample, had previous experience in more than one type of school. A small group of teachers (three per cent) had more unusual experiences to offer – work in schools overseas, in special and approved schools and in military colleges. An even smaller group (one per cent of the sample) had taught previously in junior schools only. One aspect of previous experience was deemed of special interest, i.e. whether this had involved the teaching of unstreamed groups. Of the 479 teachers in the sample, 36 per cent indicated that this was the case and indeed almost half of those teachers not at present substantially involved with mixed ability classes had experienced this form of grouping in other schools. A small number of teachers (13) deemed that their previous experience in schools with a selective intake had included the teaching of mixed ability classes. No teachers who had previously taught only in grammar schools, however, considered that they had experience of such classes (Figure 2.2A).

2.   The year groups taught by the sample

Just over two-thirds of the teachers in the sample were teaching pupils in their first year of secondary education, and of these teachers 95 per cent were involved with some mixed ability classes. A slightly higher proportion of the sample, three-quarters, were teaching in year two, and 71 per cent of such teachers taught some mixed ability groups. Seventy-seven per cent of the sample were teaching third-year pupils but the proportion of those teaching some mixed ability groups at this stage shows a further decline to 50 per cent. All except eight per cent of the sample taught pupils in the fourth and fifth years, and of those teaching these year groups 44 per cent took some mixed ability classes, whilst the majority, 56 per cent, dealt only with non-mixed ability groups. Teachers' decreasing involvement with unstreamed classes in the more senior years is illustrated in Figure 2.1.

Figure 2.1: *The proportion of teachers teaching some mixed ability or only non-mixed ability classes in each year group*

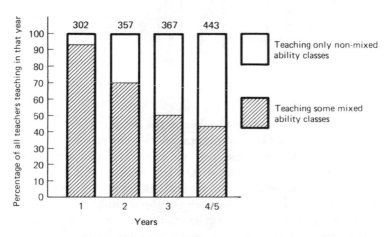

Forty-eight per cent of the teachers were involved with mixed ability groups in the lower school (i.e. years 1–3) only, whilst a further 35 per cent taught some mixed ability groups in both lower and upper (years 4 and 5) parts of the school. Six per cent of the sample (52 teachers) taught mixed ability groups only in the 4th and 5th years and 11 per cent, as already noted, were not involved with mixed ability groups at all.

Heads of department were generally less involved with mixed ability classes than other members of staff (Figure 2.2). Whilst in years 1 and 2 the disparity is small, in years 3, 4 and 5 the differences in involvement become more marked and reach a high level of statistical significance.

Figure 2.2:   *The proportion of heads of department and other members of staff teaching some mixed ability classes in each year group*

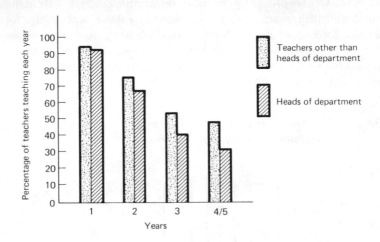

3. The subjects taught by teachers in the sample

Teachers were asked to complete a questionnaire, one part of which required them to detail the subjects and the type (i.e. mixed ability, setted, etc.) of classes taught. On the basis of this information, subjects were classified under general category headings – a considerable task in view of the diversity of the schools' curricula. Some subject areas presented particular difficulties. Humanities, for example, was found to be extremely complex, with some schools teaching it as an integrated subject in the curriculum, whilst others used it as a loose term to describe a collection of anything up to six discrete subjects. It was often found to be interchangeable with 'integrated studies', itself a term used to describe a wide range of classroom activities (AMA, 1974).

The classification eventually devised subsumed subjects under 15 main headings (Table 2.1A). Each category contains several subjects; hence any information relating to teachers in, say category 7 will refer to staff who teach sociology, as well as to those who teach history, religious education or current affairs. A consequence of this system is that it is possible for a member of staff to teach a subject – Subject 15, for example, to both mixed ability and non-mixed ability groups in one year, the explanation being that he teaches 'metalwork' to a mixed ability group whilst also teaching 'engineering drawing' to a setted group. Moreover, many teachers teach more than one subject and in order to be able to make sensible comment relating to what teachers would claim to be 'their' subject it was necessary to make a distinction between a subject taught as a 'main' subject and one taught as a 'subsidiary' subject. Since in many cases this distinction is not readily apparent, information concerning subjects taught by each teacher required careful inspection. A subject was said to be a main subject if (i) it was taught in the upper school or, if this did not apply, (ii) a clear majority of time was spent on it. Familiar patterns emerged, such as that of the teacher involved with integrated science in years 1, 2 and 3, whilst teaching physics in years 4/5. In such a case physics (14) was classified as the main subject, with integrated science (13) as the subsidiary subject. The main subjects of all except 10 teachers in the sample were identified and a description of the teachers in terms of these subjects is given in Figure 2.3.

Figure 2.3: *The distribution of teachers in the sample according to their main subject (N = 479)*

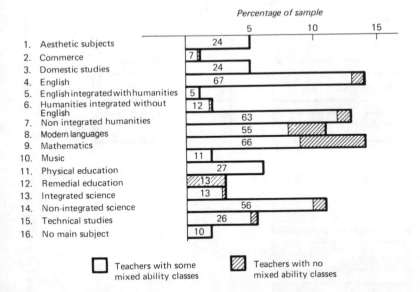

4. **Mixed ability classes, subjects and year groups**
It was reported in section 2 of this chapter that almost half of the

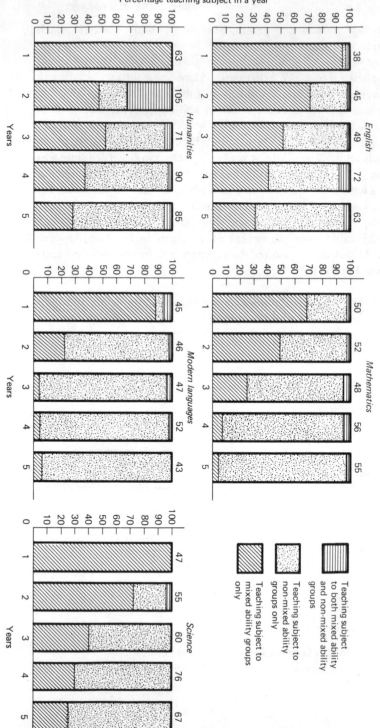

Figure 2.4: *Percentage of teachers teaching subjects to different types of teaching group in years one to five*

teachers were involved with mixed ability groups in the first three years of secondary education only, whilst just over a third (35 per cent) were teaching older pupils in mixed groupings as well. Figure 2.4 shows the extent to which teachers in selected major subject areas taught mixed ability classes in the various year groups. In the case of the humanities and science, all teachers of first-year classes were teaching the subject to mixed ability groups only, and in the other subjects – English, modern languages and mathematics the same was true for the majority of teachers. Mathematics, however, is notable as being the one first-year subject in which a considerable number of teachers (28 per cent of those teaching mathematics in this year) were involved only with non-mixed ability groups. Even modern languages which posed considerable problems for many teachers working with mixed ability groups (v Chapter 6) were taught for the most part (i.e. by 87 per cent of modern languages teachers) to unstreamed groups in year one.

A marked change, however, can be discerned in the pattern of mixed ability and non-mixed ability classes in years two and three. Seventy-one per cent of teachers involved with English in year two dealt only with mixed ability classes as compared with 95 per cent in year one. In the humanities the decline is dramatic – from 100 per cent in year one to 48 per cent in year two. Twenty-two per cent of modern languages teachers and 50 per cent of mathematics teachers in year two taught mixed ability classes only, as compared with 87 per cent and 70 per cent respectively in year one, whilst the figure for science teachers similarly decreased to 73 per cent.

In year three, of those teaching English just over half were dealing only with unstreamed groups, whilst the figure for humanities teachers remained approximately the same as in year two (52 per cent). The proportion of mathematics teachers involved only with mixed ability classes dropped, however, to under a quarter and in the case of modern languages just one of the 47 teachers of third year pupils was teaching only mixed ability groups.

Whilst mixed ability modern languages virtually disappeared in schools from the third year on and unselected mathematics groups became increasingly uncommon, a substantial though diminishing proportion of teachers of English, humanities and science continued to teach their subjects to mixed ability groups in the fourth and fifth years. Caution is however required in any investigation of grouping in the later secondary years. Most children in their third year are required to make option decisions. In many cases this has the effect of separating children into groups which are, to a certain extent, ability determined. Thus, although there may be no expressed grouping policy in the fourth and fifth year, classes described as unselected may nevertheless contain a limited range of ability.

5. Discussion

In describing the teachers who were interviewed in the course of the study, this chapter has sought to provide a context to which the comments which provide the bulk of the evidence reported in the sections which follow may be related. The sample was designed to be representative of the 29 schools participating in the project – schools which, as is apparent in the next chapter, represented a variety of differing circumstances in which mixed ability teaching may occur. The sample was not specifically designed to be representative of the total teaching population and the larger representation of male teachers in two areas has been noted, as has the under-representation of teachers on the senior teacher scale. Teachers with departmental responsibilities, however, are well represented because of the sampling strategy adopted.

There can be little doubt that we have here a sample of teachers who are exceptionally well-equipped to talk about mixed ability grouping. Not only were 403 out of the 479 teachers interviewed substantially involved with mixed ability classes, but as many as 36 per cent of the sample had had experience of teaching such classes in other schools and many of those who were not substantially involved with mixed ability groups at the time of our enquiry had none the less had experience of these in some previous teaching post.

Several points have emerged in the course of describing the sample which perhaps merit particular attention. The first concerns regional differences in staffing in terms of the balance of numbers of teachers with various lengths of teaching experience; the apparent implications of such differences for the introduction of mixed ability teaching will be explored in later chapters. Second, is the marked trend for heads of departments to be less involved with teaching mixed ability classes – particularly in the more senior years – than other staff; and third, is the substantial decline in the incidence of mixed ability grouping after the first year. Of teachers teaching the various year groups, 95 per cent taught mixed ability classes in year one, as compared with 71, 50 and 44 per cent in years two, three, four and five. The particular difficulties of teaching mathematics and modern languages to mixed ability groups are well-illustrated by the relatively lower proportions of teachers involved with such groups in all years, and the attitudes and approaches of the teachers of these and other subjects will be explored in Chapter Six.

Chapter Three

School Policy and its Implementation

'The change from a streamed to a totally unstreamed system is a major upheaval for any school and can be a traumatic experience for head, staff and pupils, not to mention parents, governors and others who are interested in the school's welfare. The manner in which the transition is effected, therefore, and in particular the kind of advance planning that is done are crucial.' (A. V. Kelly, 1978)

Why, in view of the controversy surrounding mixed ability teaching and the lack of consistent evidence as to its outcomes, do schools introduce it? Where does the initiative for its introduction lie and what are its implications for the general organization of a school? This chapter seeks to explore such questions using evidence from discussion with heads and their staffs and from documents pertinent to the organization of mixed ability teaching in their schools. In marshalling the extensive and complex body of material available, our aim has been to search out common ideas and patterns whilst highlighting issues which have emerged in particular circumstances and which may have wider relevance. The chapter is divided into a number of sections covering the procedures employed for introducing mixed ability grouping, the preparation of teachers, the involvement of parents and modifications to the organization of the timetable, staffing and school plant associated with the move to unselected groups. We begin, however, by considering reasons given for the introduction of mixed ability grouping.

1. Why mixed ability?
The initiative for abandoning forms of selective grouping came in most cases from heads (v p.28) and by far the most common reasons

24

cited by those present when their schools introduced mixed ability groups concerned the concept of a 'fresh start' and the avoidance of labelling at the outset of a child's secondary school career. Reference was made to the '*known* results of teacher expectation and attempting to predict performance at this stage', 'the halo effect', 'self-fulfilling prophecies', 'self-perpetuating labelling', 'writing children off', 'children's acceptance of a social pattern following labelling', and the need to delay emphasizing differences until as late as possible. Several heads mentioned their own experience of pupils' performance changing as they progressed through school, and others stressed the need to 'keep doors open' and provide a 'common core of learning experiences', thus avoiding 'the milk and water diet' previously offered to lower streams. A common curriculum was also necessary in the view of one head to compensate for differing primary experiences; some children were under-privileged because of the weaknesses of particular feeder schools.

Mixed ability groups were introduced for reasons which may broadly be described as 'egalitarian' in several instances; 'School resources should be made available to the individual in accordance with his rights'. 'I am a keen comprehensivist – I feel that on transition children must have equal opportunity.' Others described streaming as 'contrary to comprehensive policy', and believed it 'socially unacceptable to separate children'. The social aspect was put most strongly by those heads who had been moved to unstream by their experience of 'sink' forms – 'Unstreaming is socially desirable; you shouldn't have all the kids with dirty vests in one form. Sure, the abler would get on faster if they were streamed, but is this the acme of what we are aiming for? Basically it is a question of *objectives*' – and from the head of a former grammar school confronted with its first comprehensive intake: 'The acquisition of knowledge is not the be-all and end-all of education. Basically the decision to unstream was social and not academic.'

Nearly half the heads who had introduced mixed ability grouping to their schools emphasized the difficulty of allocating pupils to streamed groups, or even to broader bands of ability. One had systematically observed that in a three-band system where a common syllabus was taught, there was a substantial number of pupils at the top of the second band who did better than pupils in the first band, and difficulties of allocating border-line pupils, together with problems associated with transfer between streams were frequently stressed: 'You can't do it (i.e. stream) properly; you can't get the groups right.' Devious methods were sometimes employed by heads to demonstrate this to their staff (see, for instance, the example cited on p.30). The 'known' inaccuracy of predictive tests was mentioned, and several heads considered that the information received from the primary schools provided an inadequate basis for separating children in streams. The need for a period of 'diagnosis' was stressed: 'There wasn't enough information from primary schools to stream; *in any case we didn't want to act on others' information.*'

Experience of the success of mixed ability grouping within the more restricted ability range of a secondary modern school featured among the reasons given by one-third of the heads for retaining it after comprehensive reorganization. Two heads, for example, referred to their experience of fifth-year examination success among unstreamed secondary modern pupils; in one instance fourth- and fifth-year pupils had been 'mixed' with the result that some obtained O-level passes a year earlier than their grammar school counterparts. Others, though without direct experience of unstreaming, were influenced by the apparent success it had elsewhere, and some by experience of the negative effects of streaming in grammar schools where they had previously taught: 'Streaming works well for those in the top streams, but the bottom forms, even in grammar school, perform minimally.' 'I taught in a two-form entry streamed grammar school; pupils in the second stream commonly left with one or two O-levels. We then scrambled the lot and the whole school's morale went up and discipline problems vanished.'

The desire to introduce mixed ability teaching was closely linked by a small number of heads to their wish to foster the introduction of 'individualized', 'independent' or 'resource-based' learning. These classroom strategies, it was considered, could be carried out effectively in classes embracing a wide range of abilities 'without creating the social structure divisions associated with streaming'. It was among these heads, however, that most emphasis was placed on academic progress – 'my reasons were academic – I wanted a separate stream for every single child'. 'What we are striving for is the development of a learning environment which will enable young people to organize their own learning and to learn independently'; this was seen as a preparation for adult life and the need for it supported by citing examples of sixth-formers and adults, who, having been 'taught', were unable to organize their own learning. Individualized learning, which mixed ability groups rendered a necessity, was thus considered itself to be of prime importance.

In other instances mixed ability teaching was seen as part of a package. One head, for example, viewed it as part of a scheme for organizing the teaching in his school on a faculty basis. Others considered it an essential characteristic of a strong house system, where pastoral and teaching units were identical. 'I believe that school should have some influence on society; it should be con-cerned with issues such as the breakdown of the family unit. We want to use the educational system in school to enhance and strengthen the concept of the family. Because of this we strengthened the family house unit. House groups, we decided, must become learning groups. Hence we unstreamed our teaching units to correspond with the unstreamed social units.' Another head associated mixed ability teaching with the social and pastoral organ-ization as closely: 'The idea of teaching in house groups appealed just as much as mixed ability teaching. About one-third of the teaching of each first year is taken by the house tutor.'

Most of the reasons given by heads are familiar to anyone who has listened to the debate on mixed ability teaching in recent years. Many, however, still merit scrutiny. What, for example, are the implications of the concept of the 'fresh start'? Children at the age of 11 have already received six years' schooling; different aptitudes and abilities will already have emerged; different types of cur-riculum will already have been experienced – it is highly likely that some children will have started a modern language, for example, whilst others will not; girls will almost certainly have had a different curricular diet in some respects from boys. How realistic is it to ignore such variations when grouping pupils? Why just a fresh start at 11? Why is it wrong to 'label' at 11 and acceptable at 12 or 13 as happens in schools where mixed ability groups are employed for one or two years only for purposes of 'diagnosis'. What are secon-dary teachers really saying about the professionalism of their prim-ary colleagues when they assert that they do not wish to accept 'others'' judgements of pupils?

Unfortunately the relatively brief time available for discussions did not permit these and other important issues to be probed adequately, and there was the further difficulty that heads sometimes found it hard to recall all the facets of the complex set of circumstances surrounding a decision, often made some years ago, to 'go mixed ability'. Initial aims became hard to separate from subsequent desired or perceived outcomes. It is also likely that some factors affecting the decision to introduce mixed ability groups which were perceived as less acceptable were not revealed. It is interesting to note in this context that in the three instances where the desire to 'follow a fashion' was given as a reason for introducing mixed ability grouping, it was imputed to the *previous* school management. 'All the educational pundits were talking about it and he (i.e. the previous head) wanted to jump on the bandwagon'; 'My predecessor's educational philosophy was probably based on the colour supplements of the *Observer*!'

2.   How mixed ability teaching was introduced

In the paragraphs which follow the modes of introducing mixed ability grouping to schools are classified under three broad descriptions: directive, consultative and pragmatic/experimental. There is clearly overlap among these; in the first, the directive mode, the decision to introduce mixed ability groups lies wholly or mainly with the head, although we shall see that evidence of the consultative or pragmatic modes may be found in the strategies employed by him to 'sell' his policy to his colleagues. The directive mode was by far the most common, and describes what happened in over two-thirds of the schools visited. The consultative mode, as its name implies, is characterized by discussion, which may be organized on a departmental basis or use some other grouping of staff, either self-selected or chosen by virtue of particular responsibilities. Whilst the initiative in setting up such consultation might still arise from the head, a salient feature of the consultative mode is that the outcome is not predetermined; there is, in other words, a real possibility of rejecting mixed ability groups either across the board or for specific departments. The third mode of introduction, the pragmatic/experimental, describes the situation found in some schools, where mixed groupings develop piecemeal, department by department, over a period of years, or where mixed groups are introduced in one or more subjects over a period of time to see how they work. The initiative for such experiments might come from the head, senior school management, a group of staff from different disciplines or from a subject department. Some examples of each approach follow.

i. *The directive approach*

Our first example of the directive method of introducing mixed ability groups occurs in a large inner city school. This had, at the time of the enquiry, been comprehensive for some 20 years but mixed ability grouping was relatively recent, having been intro-duced some three years previously by the head a year after his appointment. The head claimed that he had decided 'completely authoritatively' that the school should be unstreamed and started with the first year, where all subjects were unstreamed. Mixed ability groups were continued into the second year where all subjects were unstreamed except languages. At the time of the interviews teaching groups were unstreamed in the first three years of the school, with the exception of languages. Initially, the head reported that 70–80 per cent of the staff were 'apprehensive'. They 'didn't see why' groups should be unstreamed, whilst the remainder were either 'hotly agin' or 'hotly for', the latter group containing 'worst of all those who espoused it for political or social reasons'. The head claimed to have played a crucial role in the preparation of teachers for the change. Teachers were sent out to primary schools to seek a basis for developing learning experience models appro-priate to secondary education, and viewings of video tapes from other schools were arranged. Time for resources development was made available, with each department in turn having a week allocated for this, during which work was set for all classes, which would be supervised by colleagues from other departments. The head went to each department in turn and discussed objectives and the roles of various staff in the development of resources. This was repeated each year for the first three years and a central repro-graphics area organized. Some three years after these changes, the head reported that in a survey carried out among staff, only one teacher had registered views antagonistic to mixed ability grouping, although he acknowledged that there were still difficulties concern-ing teachers adapting to new roles.

One of the main tasks of our enquiries was to match perception with perception, to see how far what was intended and perceived by school management found confirmation in the actions and attitudes of staff. We were able to get the views of very few of the staff present at the time mixed ability teaching was introduced because in the intervening three years a considerable number had left – the school had in fact one of the highest staff turnovers amongst those in the study. Whilst teachers who were present confirmed that mixed ability teaching was introduced as a result of the 'head's choice' or 'school policy', few were able to recollect the apparently extensive preparations made within their department for the change. We found too, that even in our sample of teachers (roughly 25 per cent) there were a number who were unconvinced as to the merits of unstreaming.

The next two examples demonstrate initiative rather than direction, with the heads concerned seeking over a considerable period of time to present to their colleagues evidence of the possible benefits of a mixed ability organization. In one case, the head claimed that he did not expect others to follow his initiative. His school, a large urban comprehensive, now has a long experience of mixed ability teaching dating back to the early 1960s when it was introduced gradually over three years. Prior to this, children on entry were given tests in English, mathematics and general knowledge, and these together with scores on a measure of verbal reasoning and weighted primary school assessments were used to allocate them to streams. However it was noted that differences within groups were as marked as those between, and each year pupils had to be transferred. The head, deciding this was nonsense, reversed the top two streams one year and 'nobody found out'. He then decided to teach his one class using a mixed ability house group and found this worked well; he was, he claimed 'more on his toes', he considered he got further in the syllabus with the abler pupils, who were stimulated into new trains of thought by questions posed by their less able counterparts, and, encouraged by his results, he invited his departmental heads to follow him. In the first year his challenge was taken up by the handicrafts, domestic science, physical education, music and religious knowledge departments. A year later, mathematics and science came in and the following year, the historians and geographers and modern linguists. Though late in coming, they were considered to be better prepared, and despite the head's commitment to mixed ability grouping in the early years of secondary schooling, he insisted that the heads of department had to be in favour before it was introduced – hence the staggering of the introduction. Neither was he in favour of continuing unstreamed groups beyond the second year, when he considered that children became 'more and more divergent'. Experiments with mixed ability groups in the third year had been discontinued.

A similar process of the head initiating experimentation occurs in our next school. Again an established comprehensive school, it moved on the appointment of the new head in the early sixties from streaming to banding, with three blocks of three parallel forms. The head felt that the case for mixed ability groups had to be demonstrated objectively to staff. Banding was a first step. Comparison of examination results indicated that if the same syllabus was taught to the top and second band there was a substantial number of pupils at the top of the second band who performed better than those at the bottom of the first. The width of the top band was accordingly increased and improvements were noted in both the performance and behaviour of the less gifted. Encouraged by this, the move was made to mixed ability groups in the first two years, and this was followed the next year by mixed groups in the first three years. The experimental nature of the new method of organization was stressed; it had to be demonstrated to work in a situation which could be construed as slightly favourable in that the school at that time did not receive the full range of ability.

The classification of these two examples as instances of the directive method is clearly open to question, and much centres on the extent to which staff were able in the first example to resist the pressure of example and in the second, to question both the introduction of the experiment and the interpretation of its working and the subsequent continuation of mixed ability grouping. As at the time of the enquiry we were asking about events which had begun some ten years previously, there were very few teachers in our sample who were present at the time in question. Those who were, however, were unanimous that unstreaming had resulted from the 'head's decree'. In the case of the first example one teacher recalled that there had been some discussion but also that 'one wouldn't have argued'.

There is no doubt as to the balance between direction and choice in the examples which follow. Located in area one, a predominantly rural area with some light industry, the schools concerned comprised a group of neighbouring schools which were reorganized as comprehensives at the same time, with their heads co-operating on policy and planning. In the words of a letter circulated to parents of new entrants in one of the schools 'the curriculum for each school has been so arranged that the schools are similar, while each school retains its own individuality. The subject syllabuses have been planned by joint working parties from the schools and are also similar.' A decision was taken by the heads of the schools involved to have mixed ability grouping 'across the board' in the first year. There was no consultation with staff. The reasons for the decision given by heads at the time of our interviews were that with the abolition of the eleven plus, there would be little information on children on transfer from primary schools, and they did not wish to replace the eleven plus by other tests.

The decision to implement mixed ability grouping at the time of comprehensive reorganization for first year pupils had markedly different implications for the schools concerned. In one, a small former secondary modern school, reorganization meant initially an intake of only 20 more children. Pupils had been allocated to 'family groups' whilst the school was still a secondary modern, and a range of subjects had been taught to O- and CSE-levels. The staff reaction to mixed ability groups being continued after reorganization was described by the head as being virtually nil: 'It was no different from what was happening before.' Subsequently the intake increased and the head at the time of interview was concerned that teaching methods had not evolved to meet the new situation.

The effects of the decision to 'go mixed ability' had more obvious and immediate effects for the reorganized former grammar school. Here, most teachers were encountering a 'new kind of child', which they had never taught before. In practical subjects and in English this presented comparatively few problems, but in mathematics and modern languages the strains were apparent within a month. Attempts were made to draw on outside experience, but visits to other schools were not particularly helpful; examples of effective mixed ability teaching could not be found, and where claims were made that it was taking place, enquiries revealed that it was with reference to a basically secondary modern intake or that some form of setting or banding was being employed. After six months' trial, it was decided to extract the 20 least able students in mathematics and French and make the other groups of equal ability. Nearly four years later when our interviewing took place, many teachers were still unhappy with having to teach the first-year pupils in mixed ability groups. The head commented that 'staff wouldn't have it in the first year if they could help it and pooh-pooh the idea of its working in other schools'. Again it was noted that 'people are still teaching homogeneous groups – there hasn't been much change in methods or materials'.

Similar difficulties were noted in another of the schools, which had developed from an amalgamation of two former secondary modern schools, both of which had been streamed before comprehensive reorganization. Mixed ability groups were introduced for all subjects in the first year, with the exception of mathematics and French, which set after one term. Second-year pupils were taught in bands or sets for all subjects except art, crafts and physical education. Again, several years after the introduction of mixed ability groups, when the research team visited the school, many staff still retained their antagonism, and in this context, staff age and stability were seen as problems. Most of the posts of responsibility on reorganization had been filled by teachers from the previous secondary schools. All the schools in the neighbourhood, and this one in particular, were characterized by a very low staff turnover: three per cent of the school's staff had left in the 1974–75 academic year, and five per cent in 1975–76. At the time of the enquiry (1975–76) only two of the 64 teachers in the school had fewer than three years' experience – the lowest incidence encountered in any school. Teachers here, as in other schools in the area were, on average, older than those in other regions studied. Both staff attitudes and staff skills presented problems; attitudes to the immediate past were slow to change, as were teaching methods, which the recently-appointed head described as 'chalk and talk', adding that what staff were really saying was, 'This is not the way I'm trained to teach or used to teaching and I want to do it my own way.' Other difficulties were mentioned; the school was described as 'not being geared to resource-based learning' and general inadequacy of financing was referred to with the qualification that 'a lot could none the less be done without money'. The desire to satisfy the 'traditional norms of parents' was also seen as hampering developments. In attempting to meet the challenges presented by having children of a wide range of ability in one class, a corporate approach was difficult because of problems of amalgamating the staffs of two schools which were 'poles apart'.

In the other two schools in the area, mixed ability groups had been employed whilst the schools were receiving a secondary modern intake. In one, a school with fewer than 600 pupils in a basically rural community, they had been introduced two years prior to reorganization and the staff were apparently happy with the new system at least in the first year where all subjects were taught to mixed ability groups. In the second year, a blocked timetable allowed departments to decide their organization, and setting was introduced for English, mathematics, modern languages and science. One problem, however, in the head's view was the relatively poor staff-pupil ratio of 1:20, to which he attributed the fact that teachers had not been able to adapt their teaching strategies and were still teaching as if in a streamed organization. This school again had a very low staff turnover (only one teacher had left in each of the years 1974–75 and 1975–76) and only a tenth had fewer than three years' teaching experience. A similarly stable and experienced staff characterized the other school, where two years' experience of mixed ability groups as a small secondary modern was followed by comprehensive reorganization and an accompanying realization of 'the magnitude of the job'. Here all subjects were taught to mixed groups in the first year, with the English, mathematics and modern languages departments introducing setting in the second year, and the science department in the third year. Staff 'prejudice' was again mentioned as a constraint, particularly in the mathematics and modern languages departments which 'hadn't really accepted it', but the head's view was that over the years '*thinking people* find solutions and the non-thinking people don't'. Lack of materials suitable for a wide range of ability and finding teacher time to 'do' innovation were also identified as constraints.

Whilst evidence of many of the difficulties encountered in this area was also found elsewhere, the schools described above perhaps provided the clearest expression of them, and indeed as is reported in Chapter Five the teachers here differed significantly from those in other areas in their attitudes towards mixed ability grouping, and were less prepared to see advantages in it. Considerable attempts had been made to prepare them for the new method of grouping; courses had been organized by the authority and inter-school work groups had met over a period of years. Yet all the heads noted failure to adopt new approaches, and this was attributed to a number of factors; first were the characteristics, in terms of length of experience, of their teaching staff coupled with the fact that very low staff turnover meant that little 'new blood' could be injected into their institutions. Lack of materials was seen as a particular problem and one which arose, not as much from lack of financial resources, as from staff reluctance or inability either to devote time to their development or to select from those published, with the change in teaching content and approach these frequently imply. It should be noted that whilst one of the schools referred to poor staffing ratio as a problem, which might explain why teachers had little time for development, in another the years after the introduction of mixed ability groups corresponded with a period of overstaffing whilst numbers built up after reorganization. It was in fact in this school, a former grammar school, where the greatest resistance to mixed ability grouping was encountered. One of the difficulties highlighted by one head was the fact that the community served by the schools was relatively isolated and institutions which might support innovation, such as colleges and departments of education were some distance away. Even when allowances for this were made, however, he and other heads were critical of the fact that these institutions had been very slow to provide teachers with the kind of help needed.

ii. The consultative approach
The first example of an approach to the introduction of mixed ability grouping markedly different from those outlined above is that of a school which opened as a new comprehensive in an 'overspill' area in September 1970. It began with an intake of 170 pupils and 12 staff, and its catchment included two private housing estates and two urban villages, with predominantly private housing designed for workers in the new firms. Before the school opened a number of preliminary staff meetings were held and two of the major policy decisions reached were that the pastoral structure should be horizontal and that the timetable be devised to allow mixed ability groups or setting. At subsequent staff conferences it emerged that all departments were prepared to try mixed ability grouping and that some, including the mathematics department, thought that it could be carried through until the end of the fifth year. In the event maths sets were found to be necessary from the fourth year on, and modern languages introduced setting after the first year. This latter decision was resented by some staff, who felt that the modern languages department had 'let them down'. However, the general approach to mixed ability teaching in the school

was pragmatic – 'if it didn't work we'd change' – and the linguists had found that the nature of their subject, with its growing emphasis on grammatical construction, combined with the fact that they '*had* to do class teaching', made mixed ability grouping impracticable after the early stages. At the time of the enquiry, the school had nearly 1,500 pupils and its initial entry had just completed their first public examinations, the results of which had been encouraging; the proportion of pupils obtaining five or more O-levels at grades A, B or C, was estimated at 25 per cent above the national average and virtually no child had left without an academic qualification.

The school was fortunate in that it never experienced difficulty in attracting staff and indeed in its initial recruitment had received more than 1,200 applications for its 12 posts. Such constraints as were identified related to a need for more ancillary staff and, particularly, for staff for reprographics. Other difficulties centred on the 'enormous' amount of preparation time needed, a problem which had increased as the school roll built up and the early days of over-staffing passed, and it was no longer possible to allow for timetabled departmental meetings.

More formalized procedures of consultation characterized the next school in this section. This had developed from a secondary modern school where some mixed ability groups had been used and which became comprehensive in 1972. In the year prior to reorganization, the form of grouping to be used in the new school was discussed in a staff conference and four working parties established dealing with (a) curriculum, (b) organization, (c) social and pastoral care and (d) links with primary schools. Among their recommendations were that the timetable should be blocked, that mixed ability groups should be used where possible, that a resource centre be established and that an extra teaching centre be set up for pupils with special needs. Since these early discussions, the original 21 staff had been joined by a further 50 and the working parties had continued and at the time of the enquiry involved around three-quarters of the staff, with each group electing its own convenor who reported to the head each week.

Difficulties in using broad ability groups were encountered in modern languages and mathematics, the first of which set after year one and mathematics after year two. Science used mixed ability groups in years 1–3, and English, the humanities, creative studies and physical education throughout the five years although it should be noted that at the time of this study the fifth year was not comprehensive.

The decision on going comprehensive to organize pupils in mixed ability groups had been influenced by the fact that those teachers who had witnessed the introduction of such groups into the old secondary modern school had noted beneficial changes in the school's social climate. There were, however, problems associated with this form of grouping, the most important perhaps being providing for the entire ability range, particularly for the least able who could take up 'a disproportionate amount of time', and for the 'extrovert non-academic'. There were constraints imposed by the nature of the building and it was not always possible to arrange departmental rooms together. Again the difficulties of finding ancillary staff to develop a resource centre were mentioned, and the provision of adequate staff training was also raised.

iii. The pragmatic – experimental approach

In the school we shall now consider, in contrast to the previous example, there was no general discussion about the adoption of mixed ability groups. As a secondary modern school prior to reorganization in 1972, it had used mixed ability in some subjects – design, music, mathematics and physical education and had established a good academic reputation with some children studying subjects to GCE Advanced level. It had been the experience that examination courses attracted children 'who wanted to have a go' and indeed some children regarded as less able academically had been successful at O-level. After reorganization, the school, which was located in a rapidly-growing country town which served as a 'dormitory town' for an overspill development, had a wide range of ability and a very high proportion of children from a service base who formed a transitory population. Departments were left to decide which form of grouping to adopt, as it was felt that the departmental heads (who came mainly from grammar schools) were new and unknown, as indeed were the children. The head's view was that mixed ability groups were perfectly acceptable if the teachers in a department had enthusiasm for them and were prepared to plan. In connection with the latter, the need for modular material and individualized teaching was stressed, as was the desirability of keeping classes small – no larger than 25. At the time of our investigation the English and modern languages department had opted for mixed ability groups in the first year, science for the first two years, mathematics for the first three years and the design, music and physical education departments for all year groups – a degree of flexibility which substantiated the head's view that teachers should teach in a way they believed in.

In addition to resources, which here as in other schools were cited as a difficulty, the problem of ensuring that all children, particularly the *less* able, were 'stretched' in mixed ability groups was referred to, as were problems relating to the attitudes of pupils in the middle secondary years: 'No matter what one does one does not influence enough the anti-social sub-culture that seems to emerge from the third year onwards. You can give the opportunity but there is no way you can ensure that all children take advantage'. Curiously, the head did not think that the dropping of mixed ability grouping in most subjects by the end of the third year strengthened that sub-culture, although he did see one of the outcomes of mixed ability grouping as diminishing 'social structure divisions'.

The final example is of a school where, following discussions, mixed ability groups were introduced gradually over a period of years. When the school became comprehensive in 1969, pupils were organized in bands, but a study group of any staff interested in exploring the implications of introducing mixed ability groups was set up, and two years later the first of these groups was introduced. Initially, two of the first-year classes were mixed ability, the remainder being banded. The following year all first-year pupils were organized in mixed groups and the two second-year classes, which had been unstreamed in the first year, remained so. In the third year following the introduction of mixed ability teaching all first- and second-year classes were unstreamed. At the time of our investigations, all subjects were taught in mixed ability groups in the first two years, and English, geography, history, music, religious education, physical education, boys' and girls' craft retained mixed classes in the third year. Setting was used in the third year for mathematics, science, languages and art. Again the attitudes of staff were identified as all important and the presence of a high proportion of experienced teachers from the former grammar school was seen as a distinct advantage – 'they do even better in the present situation'. Problems in the head's view included the identification of objectives, assessment – 'matching the child and the learning opportunity', and teaching style – reference being made to a lot of 'dubious class teaching'.

These examples illustrate the variety of ways in which mixed ability grouping may be introduced; they show its introduction by heads operating without consultation; by heads who, whilst the initiators, sought by example or by carefully-planned experiment to convince their staff; by groups of teachers meeting to decide their school's policy on grouping and by subject departments exercising autonomy over their particular grouping practices. The examples demonstrate how similar modes of introduction may have very differing consequences according to the different histories and emphases of the schools involved. Hence we see how on reorganization in one geographical area the imposition of mixed ability grouping without consultation apparently had little effect in a school which had unstreamed as a secondary modern and where the size of the new comprehensive intake was small. In the former grammar school, however, where staff were encountering children of a different ability from that to which they were accustomed, and in the school formed from two previously streamed secondary moderns where difficulties of achieving cohesion between the staffs of the former schools were considerable, severe problems rapidly emerged and persisted at least till the time of enquiry some years later. In this area particular constraints arose from low staff turnover and the comparatively lengthy teaching experience of many teaching staff. A very different situation may be noted in the case of the new comprehensive in a recently formed overspill area, where it had been possible to recruit from a wide field staff who at least were sympathetic to comprehensive education and who later opted as a group to try a mixed ability organization. Our study, then, follows others in accentuating the importance of staff attitudes and staff commitment. Further factors are suggested as having a bearing on the effectiveness with which mixed ability teaching can be carried out: the availability of resources; the existence of adequately equipped and staffed reprographics services; the availability of time for preparation and discussion; the size of classes and the provision of adequate departmental accommodation.

Finally, the examples appear to point to a need for flexibility in grouping policy and here again variety among the schools is apparent, with some opting from the outset for departmental discretion on how pupils are grouped and others having flexibility thrust upon them when attempts at mixed ability teaching in some subject areas were deemed to have failed.

Preparing teachers for mixed ability teaching

Heads were generally agreed that mixed ability teaching required new methods in the classroom, but few considered the opportunities offered either in or out of school for teachers to prepare for these to be adequate. The Assistant Masters Association (1974) made the point that 'the teaching of mixed ability groups is potentially more fraught with danger in the hand of the inexpert or unwilling teachers . . .' and questioned the lack of training in this area. With regard to pre-service training, information from the teachers in the sample substantiated this lack. A small number (eight per cent) had received no professional training at all. Of those who had received training, 65 per cent indicated that this had involved no aspects specific to dealing with mixed ability groups. In total, 67 per cent of the whole sample of teachers had entered the teaching profession unprepared for teaching unselected groups.

Those teachers who had received some initial training for mixed ability classes varied considerably in their appraisal of its usefulness. Training was reported as consisting variously of timetabled lectures, discussion, study of teaching methods and preparation of courses of study. Some teachers had been helped considerably by talks given by local teachers on approaches to mixed ability teaching and by sample lessons, and particular mention was made of the confidence gained by training which had included remedial work. Many, however, were critical that not enough practical guidance was given and comments frequently drew attention to the 'theoretical bias' of the courses and to 'limited instruction due to tutors' lack of experience.' A teacher from area five summed up his comments by writing: 'The term mixed ability was used a lot but I don't remember anyone saying anything particularly useful.' Teachers in one school considered that the lack of practical training experienced by many students was likely to continue by reason of the college's reluctance to place any but its 'worst' students in the school because its mixed ability classes offered few opportunities for assessing didactic teaching. Teachers with junior/secondary or junior training however tended to have a more favourable view of their initial training in mixed ability work.

One of the main ways of preparing teachers for teaching groups with a wide range of ability in recent years has been the in-service course. Reporting on its survey conducted in 1972–3, the Assistant Masters Association found very little evidence of such courses, with only ten of the 64 schools studied indicating 'some activity'. In our sample, 40 per cent of those teachers currently substantially involved with mixed ability groups and 30 per cent of those concerned with non-mixed ability groups had attended in-service courses pertinent to mixed ability teaching. It was apparent that attendance at courses was not comparable throughout the five areas studied. Of staff interviewed in area 4, only 27 per cent had attended such courses whilst in area 1 the figure was 62 per cent. The proportion in areas 2, 3 and 5 were 37, 46 and 35 per cent respectively. Fifty-five per cent of the heads of department interviewed had attended an in-service course with elements relating directly to mixed ability teaching as compared with 30 per cent of other staff. Of the former, just over a quarter attended as organizers or tutors, the remaining three-quarters as participants.

The nature of in-service courses attended varied considerably, from short sessions after school to month-long residential courses. Course providers included the Department of Education and Science, the Local Education Authorities, subject associations, the National Union of Teachers, University Departments of Education, the Advisory Centre for Education and Teachers' Centres. Several teachers, however, expressed exasperation with courses that were either irrelevant or not sophisticated enough to be practically useful. One member of staff wrote: 'I went to the course hoping to learn, and ended up teaching others!' Many teachers, moreover, felt that such courses could only serve to stimulate discussion, and that more immediate help was gained from talking to, and observing, individual teachers. As with courses in initial training, teachers commented on the limited content: 'Almost the sole concern was the production of worksheets!'

Considerable criticism of local in-service courses came also from the local heads: 'Who amongst the advisory service has taught recently and successfully in a mixed ability situation?'; 'Advisers are grossly overworked; their attempts to contribute have been without expertise'; 'The courses fall down through a lack of speakers who can say anything significant'. In the circumstances, most schools relied on their own resources and the most common form of preparation for teaching unstreamed groups was that organized by the schools themselves on either a departmental or, rarely, a whole-school basis, the latter taking the form of one or two day conferences. There were also examples of timetable modifications to allow faculties in turn to spend two days considering and preparing strategies and resources and of a formalized scheme of inter-departmental observations to enable teachers in different subject disciplines to learn from one another; three schools included preparation for teaching mixed ability groups in their induction programmes for probationers. There can be little doubt, however, that constraints of time and available expertise meant that the approaches most teachers employed in their mixed ability teaching were acquired 'on the job'. Some heads considered that in any case, this had to be so: 'A lot has to be unplanned . . . much of the training for mixed ability teaching concerns teachers getting out of the "box concept" and learning to relate to their colleagues.' Indeed in six of the schools, no arrangements for any preparation for teaching mixed ability groups had been made and to the heads' knowledge there had been no courses available to teachers within the authority. 'We hope – possibly naïvely – that staff will learn as they go along,' reported the head of one such school.

The extent to which staff substantially involved with mixed ability groups at the time of our investigation had received training specifically in mixed ability methods may be summarized as follows:

	No.	%
No training for mixed ability work	153	38
Pre-service training only	82	20
In-service training only	114	28
Pre-service and In-service training	47	12
No information on training available	7	2
	403	100

4.   The introduction of mixed ability grouping and parents

The final aspect of the introduction of mixed ability teaching to be considered is the methods used by schools to make parents aware of how pupils were grouped. The phrase, '*make aware*' should be noted; in no case were parents' views sought concerning the grouping practices to be adopted.

Schools, without exception, held a meeting for the parents of new entrants prior to the autumn term and in all cases reference was made to the schools' grouping practices. Heads reported little parental reaction at this stage – probably because few parents want to be identified as being 'bolshy' from the start, but also perhaps in some cases because the implications of whatever phraseology was used, were not fully understood. This was the view of one head who stated that 'It is all so complicated that parents don't really understand it. Some staff don't either.' It is clear that a variety of phrases was used to describe mixed ability groups – in one case, for example, what parents were actually told was that their children would be taught in *house* groups – 'it dawns on them gradually what this means'. In another, they were told that children would be in 'equal' groups, and the transitoriness of the whole arrangement was often stressed: 'We make it clear that the kids will be set after year one'; 'We emphasize that by the time a child reaches the fifth year he will either have been selected or selected himself'.

Half the schools made reference in their prospectuses or in an initial letter to parents to the fact that children would be taught in mixed ability groups. Sometimes this was clearly spelt out:

'Throughout their first year in the school pupils will be taught in all subjects in their 'mixed ability' tutor groups.'
'For the first two years, when attached to the Lower School, all pupils pursue a common curriculum. All teaching takes place in mixed ability groups for all subjects in the first year, although some setting is arranged in the second year for mathematics and modern languages.'

In other schools, the description of the arrangements for grouping pupils were more obscure:

'The school does not practice a rigid policy of streaming at any level except where it is appropriate.' (All classes in the first two years in this school were, in fact, mixed ability.)
'A similar course in all general secondary subjects is taken by the first year with the exception that a small number of pupils requiring additional help with basic reading skills have more integrated subject studies initially. On entering the second year, pupils continue to be taught in house and tutor groups and to progress in a wide range of subjects. In the third year, pupils are placed in forms or sets which will permit appropriate studies to continue according to their previous rate of progress. . . .'
'The first and second years' programme is broadly-based and makes it possible for pupils to be introduced to as many subjects

as possible. These years, therefore, tend to be diagnostic. Boys and girls work in their house groups for several subjects and for others pupils are taught in groups or sets according to their attainment.'

'Pupils on entering the school are placed in one of ten parallel forms and pursue a common course for the first three years.'

Parents, unfamiliar with words and phrases such as 'diagnostic grouping' – 'setting', 'parallel forms' – or even 'streaming' – might well have had difficulty in interpreting some of the above. In half the schools, however, there were even fewer clues as to how teaching groups were organized, the topic being either not mentioned at all or sparse and general information given: 'All pupils follow a similar course'; 'pupils are taught in their tutor groups' – 'the timetable is geared to the needs of pupils of all abilities'.

The schools were almost equally divided between those where some adverse comment on mixed ability grouping had been received from parents, and those where there had been no reaction or, in one case, favourable comment ('most parents are comforted that their children are not pre-judged'). Where adverse comment was raised it came in nearly all cases from more socially advantaged families and from parents of academically able children. One head who described his school as having a wide ability range and a 'good professional element' reported how at the initial parents' evening, he either had to 'play the mixed ability bit down' or else 'go for the hard sell'. A crucial component of the hard sell was that options were setted later and this persuaded parents to accept mixed groups in the first year. Current reports in the media of the apparent failures of progressive education had made his job more difficult; it had become important that mixed ability teaching should not become identified with 'progressivism' and that was one reason why the school retained Latin. Other heads reported alarm from the parents of bright children, who asked questions such as, 'Why are they being held back?' and who expressed fears that the school was going to 'teach them as if they were remedial'. In other cases, heads considered parents' fears did not concern academic progress so much as resentment at their children 'mixing with those dreadful council house children'. In most schools, however, misgivings were restricted to relatively few parents and a number of heads reported that, as the new system had become established, expressions of parental anxiety had decreased.

5. Changes in organization associated with mixed ability teaching
An important part of the discussions with heads concerned administrative changes which had been implemented in their schools and which they perceived as associated in some measure with the adoption of mixed ability grouping – changes concerning the organization of the timetable, staffing, the use of school buildings and the relationship between subject departments. In some instances, heads found it difficult to isolate changes associated with mixed ability grouping from those associated with comprehensive reorganization or with particular curricular developments; they could not, in short, be certain that such changes would not have occurred regardless of the grouping system employed. Others were wary lest they might be seen to be prescribing essential requirements for the successful organization of mixed ability teaching and stressed, first the unique circumstances of each school and second, the desirability of a piecemeal approach: 'Schools need to *grow* into needs; it is not necessary to start with everything. They have to perceive a lack before they can utilize a facility properly when they have it.'

In the paragraphs which follow we consider aspects of the schools' organization with particular reference to any modifications occasioned by or associated with changes in grouping policy.

i. The organization of curricular time

(a) Length of teaching period
The need for time to marshal resources at the beginning and end of lessons prompted a number of schools to review the length of their teaching periods. Some schools retained the 35-minute (or, more rarely, the 45-minute) period as the basic unit of teaching time, but increased the number of double periods. Others moved to 'double' periods, usually of 70 minutes as the basic units, and in some instances, introduced 'quadruple' periods, for subjects such as integrated practical subjects and combined maths and science. In some schools, modern languages, and, less commonly, mathematics received exceptional treatment, being allocated more periods of shorter duration. 'Tolerance' limits for modern languages in particular, showed considerable variation; in some schools 70-minute periods were employed for all lessons, in others, one such double period was deemed the maximum that could be sustained, whilst others found anything but single periods of 35–40 minutes impracticable.

Getting the period length right clearly presented a number of schools with a problem, and there was evidence of experimentation with various period lengths within a relatively short space of time (in one case, two years). Several schools, for example, which had changed to 70-minute periods, found these to be too long and were, at the time of enquiry, experimenting with periods of one hour's duration. It had been found that the 20-period week left 'too little room for manoeuvre' and it was hoped that a week of 25 shorter periods would provide greater flexibility and enable more frequent contact with pupils in some subjects. There was evidence of some reluctance on the part of teachers to accept longer teaching units. One head reported 'no takers' for a move from a five- to four-period day; another, rejection of a quadruple period for integrated humanities. Both offered the same interpretation that 'many teachers have no idea of the need to adjust teacher time to mixed ability methods'. The central themes running through the discussions with heads on length of teaching period were (a) the varying requirements of different subjects and (b) the need to achieve a balance between frequency of contact on the one hand and units which were sufficiently long to enable resource-based methods to be employed, on the other.

(b)   'Blocking' the timetable

Almost half the schools arranged their timetables in blocks of time for each subject (or group of subjects) across a year group. This was seen as enabling departmental staff to teach as a team if they so wished, as facilitating the deployment of resource materials, and also in some cases as providing the opportunity for departments to group children as they wished.

(c)   Re-allocation of time between subjects

In some schools integrated studies were introduced (v p.50), and changes in the relative amounts of time given to the various subject components – if these remained distinct – could not be assessed. Apart from this, only one example was found of a school where time was taken from one subject area and given to another (presumably a delicate exercise in most schools), and this involved more time being given to science 'because they had to cater now for less able pupils' at the expense of craft subjects.

(d)   Allocation of time for departmental discussion

Only four schools allocated time for departmental discussion. One of these allocated 75 minutes each five day week and another, a 70-minute period in each school week of ten days. In a third school, where teachers generally had three non-teaching periods, faculties were invited to arrange time for discussion; only two, however, managed to do so and this scheme was not seen as being practical 'across the board'. In the fourth school, pupils went home early on one afternoon each week, releasing all staff for departmental discussion. Some schools, where the introduction of mixed ability teaching was coincidental with reorganization, had been able to arrange time for departmental meetings initially, before the school roll grew and there was relative overstaffing, but had later to give it up. By far the most common practice was for departments to meet outside curricular time, in the lunch hour or after school, and whilst this was mostly regretted by heads, there was some evidence in the smaller schools that timetabled departmental meetings were seen as unnecessary.

ii. Staffing

Staffing developments fell into two categories; (a) those associated with the production and management of resources and (b) those related to changes in role arising from the adoption of mixed ability grouping and other developments seen as being closely associated with it.

Concerning the first of these, five schools had appointed technicians (in two instances on a part-time basis) to man their resource centres. A further school re-allocated its non-teaching staff to enable one of its clerical assistants to undertake training in reprographics with an offset litho firm and return to operate a reprographics unit. An example of more extensive direction of staff into the management and production of resources occurred in a comprehensive school of some 1,500 pupils which had introduced mixed ability teaching in 1972, with the encouragement of a head whose prime interest was in resource-based learning. As the school grew and the numbers of staff increased, care was taken to ensure the adequate staffing of the school's resources; a senior teacher was appointed with specific responsibility for these and two librarians, with a technical resources assistant and a video assistant eventually completing the resources team. This school, however, was unique among those visited; the common cry was for 'more and better resources' and for ancillary staff who could assist in producing and organizing them.

Changes in the roles of staff – and we are not at this point referring to the teachers' role in the classroom – generally arose from developments which were concurrent with the introduction of mixed ability grouping and regarded as part and parcel of the 'mixed ability package'. In a number of schools, for example, the introduction of mixed ability grouping was accompanied by a revision of pastoral structure, with vertical house groupings giving way to horizontal, so that the mixed ability classes also became the pastoral units. Some heads as noted previously placed as much or more emphasis on the pastoral developments as on changes in the structure of teaching groups, with mixed ability grouping being viewed as a means of strengthening the tutorial system. Whilst most schools tended to align pastoral and teaching groups, there was however in the group of schools studied an example of a school which retained its belief in the value of the vertical house group, not used for teaching, but which mediated the school's ethos and discipline.

Another development which in some few schools was viewed as a natural associate of mixed ability grouping and which affected staff roles was the introduction of faculties or schemes for integrating various areas of the curriculum. The implications of these innovations are discussed in a separate section (v p.50).

There appeared to be little change in heads' criteria for making appointments associated with the mode of grouping adopted. When asked whether experience with mixed ability groups was something they looked for when selecting staff, a number pointed out that such experience was difficult to find and it was only recently that sufficient applicants had been available to enable them to consider a recruitment policy at all. A number said they looked for experience in comprehensive schools, but most set aside experience of any specific type in favour of personal and academic qualities. 'If a teacher is good, he is good in any sphere'; 'the first essential is to have a person of vigour, stature and sense; a person of calibre and worth rapidly makes up for lack of experience in a certain technique'; 'we look for good intelligence and interesting people, for a basis on which to build; you can teach people to have a heart but you can't give them a brain'. An element of caution was evident in some of the heads' comments: 'We don't want zealots and whilst it is unlikely that someone unsympathetic to mixed ability teaching would be appointed, we would not appoint anyone who wanted to teach mixed groups throughout the age range.' A number of heads preferred to recruit probationers whenever possible and 'train them up' for promotion. Hence although heads frequently referred to 'mixed ability teaching' as a particular kind of teaching, involving a distinct approach, contrasting it with 'teaching mixed ability groups', competence in such an approach was clearly considered to be something which an able teacher could acquire within the context of the school.

iii. Use of plant

Modifications to the ways in which schools deployed their buildings in order to meet the needs of mixed ability groups included:
(1) the formation of suites of rooms for departments.
(2) the establishment of resource centres.
(3) the creation of reprographics units.
(4) the departure from the traditional 'closed' classroom.

In many of the schools prior to the introduction of mixed ability teaching, 'the teachers moved and the classes stayed still'. Now, with the increased need to be close to a wide range of resources, many schools were seeking to allocate rooms to departments, with each department having a room to house its materials and in which to hold discussions. Often such resource rooms were little more than large cupboards – the old departmental stock room with a new name, the departmental resource centre. The centralized resource centre serving all departments found relatively few supporters among our schools. Buildings spread over a wide site were seen to make this impracticable in some schools, and where such resource centres were used by pupils the problem arose of these being able to accommodate only a few pupils at a time: 'People can't use the centre; it holds 40 children out of 1,500.' Other heads simply did not see the value of such centralization. 'I nibbled at a resource centre, but we don't have a room or a person. It is rubbish to say you need a resource centre for mixed ability teaching to work.'

The need for a reprographics unit, however, was widely recognized, although only a quarter of the schools visited had managed to allocate space for one and furnish it extensively with offset litho, photocopier, stencil cutter, video recording equipment, etc. For a number of schools it was a case of building up bit by bit and even a school which was in comparison with many others lavishly equipped reported that the number of materials waiting to be produced was embarrassing. Not surprisingly, a wide disparity in the quality of school-produced materials was evident, with many teachers producing materials in handwriting and duplicating by Banda.

The departure from the traditional 'closed' classroom was relatively rare and, as might be expected, featured in the new purpose-built schools, or in schools where major structural alterations had been carried out. Removable partitions were a major feature of the design in such schools – 'everything is designed to *make* staff work together', 'a class in a box is no good; the pedagogy is related to the building'. The few schools which wished or were able to experiment with these more flexible structures tended to see them as necessary for team teaching and for the integration of subject disciplines, rather than as specifically necessary for mixed ability teaching: 'The association is indirect; it is the result of the development of a wider philosophy of education.'

iv.   The relationship between subject disciplines

Over half the schools visited had some examples of integration among subject disciplines. Most common was combined science in the first two or three years of secondary school, which in many cases had been introduced before changes in pupils grouping procedures. Next, in terms of frequency, came humanities, followed by design and creative studies. There were several examples of integrated courses being offered in the fourth or fifth years – e.g. a health education course offered partly by biology and home economics departments; one in engineering by physics and handicraft departments, and a project technology course offered by physics, mathematics and computer studies departments.

Integration, however, was not generally viewed as part and parcel of mixed ability teaching; indeed there was evidence of considerable prosaicism in the approach of some heads: 'Some departments are efficient, others inefficient. Amalgamation is an expedient to cope with personal weakness.' It was also introduced in one school to cope with staff shortages. Several schools had tried to introduce integrated courses, but had given them up. In two such schools 'a bad appointment' was diagnosed as the source of failure; in another, a clash of personalities. A further school had tried to get the English, geography, history and religious education departments together, principally to reduce the number of teachers first year children met, but the scheme collapsed through staff antagonism: 'They found every possible reason why it couldn't be done.' Over a quarter of the schools had no integrated subjects, and generally questioned their value. 'Departments accept mixed ability teaching more easily than mergers'; 'there is a fear that the more able will lose out with integration – a subject approach is more appropriate'.

Only five schools grouped subject departments into faculties, and in two, such grouping had preceded the introduction of mixed ability teaching; in the others it was not viewed as a direct result of such an introduction although it was considered that it facilitated the kind of teaching which mixed ability groups required. In one school, faculties were seen as a remedy for 'the unhappy experiences of fragmentation'. Teaching, in the view of the head, was a 'public and corporate activity rather than private and individual. The latter model is not a progressive dynamic. The teacher can reduce his expectations because only he and his private group can see what he is doing. I want teachers to produce and evaluate materials together and to teach in front of each other.' Other heads also saw in faculties a means of making it easier for teachers to work in teams and share materials, with the faculty in one instance being described as 'a resource framework which stimulated creativity'. They also made it possible to limit the number of teachers which new pupils came in contact with if effective integration among the various constituent disciplines was achieved. Integration was not however always seen as the end or the natural consequence of a faculty structure; in one school its main function was simply to facilitate organization so that the head was dealing with a small group of senior staff who could go back 'with executive power' to their sub-groups. This was considered a more effective means of administration than attempting to discuss school policy with a group of over twenty departmental heads.

Most heads of schools were opposed to the idea of faculties and their objections may be summarized as follows:
(a) problems associated with the role of the faculty head.
(b) difficulties arising from perceived loss of status by other staff.
(c) concern over maintaining academic standards.
(d) problems of recruitment.
(e) the difficulties experienced by teachers in 'switching departments'.
(f) the difficulty of finding sensible groupings of subjects.

From a volume of comment, the following extracts from discussions with heads illustrate the points above:

'We tried to introduce faculties for humanities and for general science and mathematics. It was clear at the interviews that I didn't know what I wanted and the candidates didn't know either. We were looking for paragons that didn't exist so we called it a day.'

'Initially we tried breaking down subject barriers and appointed a director of humanities. It was a flop; if you want decent subject specialists you have to maintain subject borderlines. We now avoid the disappointment of supermen.'

'It's simply a bandwagon. We looked at places that did it and we didn't like it. Departments will not be integrated – they all build empires. You can talk integration but it won't work.'

'Departments should be numerous and small. One poor person can do a hell of a lot of damage. We have very few outstanding people even in heads of departments posts.'

'We tried. We succeeded with science but failed with humanities. There is a lot of subject insularity and teachers find it hard to switch departments. Too many teachers are concerned with what is best for *me*.'

'Different departments have different views. We didn't want a drop in standards and thought that individual disciplines might lose quality if brought together.'

'It's sometimes difficult to know where to put subjects. Music for example began in the same group as physical education and ended up with heavy craft!' (From the head of school which had faculties.)

'Natural links between subjects exist. Once these are institutionalized they become harder to achieve. By sacrificing a few powerful people you gain a lot from all sorts of people talking in different directions. Practically there are problems; faculty heads are difficult to recruit and some departments are natural ivory towers. Basically teachers are not a very distinguished profession – not geniuses. The bigger things become to run, the more exceptional people you need.'

It was evident from the comments of the heads of the few schools where faculties were viewed as a means towards integration that teachers required experience and training both in an inter-disciplinary approach and in a different role: 'Faculties tend to be insular in the same way as the old subject departments. There is not enough thinking about the nature of the faculty or about broader problems – remedial education, the basic elements of the curriculum, the provision of new learning experiences, the proportion of staff who should be deployed in a particular subject area in any year, etc.'

In short, the problems concerned with the establishment of faculties, and indeed in more modest levels of integration of subjects were seen by most heads as substantial and in only a few instances were they viewed as necessary for the effective operation of mixed ability teaching.

6. Discussion

This chapter has sought to examine reasons why schools adopt mixed ability grouping, the modes of its introduction and its implications for various aspects of school organization, and in so doing has presented a *potpourri* of aims and practice. Its intention has been to highlight issues of importance in the running of schools where mixed ability groups are employed, and to suggest a range of questions which those concerned with school management might ask about their own institutions. In all its sections it has demonstrated the variety of objectives, styles of management and organizational strategies found in schools; this variety defies summary and again emphasizes the difficulties of making global statements in relation to mixed ability teaching. There are some common threads; a degree of consensus, for example, is evident in some of the stated reasons for its adoption – that children should have the opportunity at the outset of their secondary education to start afresh and that labelling be avoided and opportunities kept open for as long as possible. The difficulties of allocating pupils to streamed groups also featured prominently among the reasons for rejecting these and other forms of selective grouping.

A feature in over two-thirds of the schools was that mixed ability grouping was introduced by methods which we have broadly classified as 'directive', with the head as initiator, staff choice minimal or absent and no consultation of parents. Readers will form their own judgements concerning the relative merits of the modes of introduction outlined in Section 2 of this chapter. Inevitably, in a series of brief thumb-nail sketches, space has not permitted the inclusion of detail which might serve to deepen such judgements. Clearly, however, the role of the head in introducing and fostering innovation is a crucial issue in this as in other aspects of school organization and activity, and whilst it is not the intention here to suggest that one style of management is necessarily in all circumstances better than others, the examples provide important pointers as to those factors which might be associated with the effective introduction and operation of mixed ability grouping. These, together with others culled from the evidence in succeeding chapters, will be discussed in the concluding chapter of the report.

In the actual implementation of their grouping policies, schools demonstrated a variety of procedures for arranging the timetable and curriculum, although in the latter case some degree of consensus emerged concerning the difficulties associated with the integration of subject disciplines. There was also a fair measure of common ground concerning the constraints identified by heads on the effective operation of mixed ability teaching. The production and organization of resources featured prominently among these, with emphasis on the lack of materials suitable for teaching a wide ability range and on the difficulties of producing quality materials in quantity without adequate ancillary staff. Many schools also encountered problems where the school building did not allow the organization of departmental rooms *en suite* ('many teachers end up like bedouins') and storage facilities were inadequate. Class size was also mentioned frequently, particularly in area two, where classes of 36 were common.

By far the most frequently stressed constraint however concerned teaching methods – 'We teach mixed ability groups but we do not do mixed ability teaching'. Many of the problems identified by heads are those identified by the teachers themselves and these are reported fully in Chapters Five and Six. They include the formulation of objectives, organizing the classroom so that each child can be given the attention he requires, extending the able and catering for the less able ('the assumption is that in secondary schools people can read'). Heads emphasized the pressures which mixed ability teaching put on staff and that its success or failure depended on their abilities. There was some pessimism concerning the latter: 'We make great demands on staff who are seldom above average calibre'; 'We are demanding of teachers a level of dedication and competence that doesn't exist'; 'The biggest variable is the teacher; the biggest constraint the ability of the teacher'; 'Many teachers lack the academic tradition which would enable them to ensure that the most able are extended'.

The attitudes of teachers were also frequently identified as obstructing the development of effective mixed ability work; reference was made to their 'natural inhibitions', 'prejudice', 'conservatism', to an inability to respond creatively to change ('they are conditioned to receive tablets and implement them'), and also to the fact that many teachers were satiated ('punch-drunk') with all the innovations of recent years. A commonly-reported constraint was that teachers found it difficult to break away from former habits of isolation and work together in new roles. Evidence of particular problems was found in schools where mixed ability teaching was introduced in newly-amalgamated schools where the staffs were 'poles apart', and where some teachers were meeting children of an ability level not previously encountered. Difficulty in finding time and the expertise to prepare teachers for approaches required in teaching unstreamed groups was widely reported, with advisers and the staffs of colleges and Departments of Education frequently being viewed as less experienced in these than members of the schools' staffs. A relatively high percentage (40 per cent) of teachers had attended in-service courses designed to help them in teaching mixed ability groups, but many were critical of their usefulness.

Evidence from heads has formed the basis of much of this chapter; in most cases, we have seen that the introduction of mixed ability teaching derived from their initiative. It is perhaps fitting as a conclusion to a chapter which has focused on policy and its implementation and as a counterbalance to heads' reported comments in the previous paragraph that we end by quoting one head who placed the responsibility for the effective operation of mixed ability teaching not so much on teachers or advisers or those involved in teacher education, as on *himself*: 'The crucial factor', he emphasized, 'is the *organization* and *management* of the school.'

Chapter Four

Allocating Pupils to Teaching Groups

1. Creating mixed ability classes

We now move on to examine first the various methods used by schools to place children in teaching groups and second, to consider some of the issues associated with providing for pupils with special needs.

This might be considered one of the most crucial tasks for any school confronted with a new intake, be it the intention to allocate pupils to streams or to groupings embracing a wider range of ability. Some heads, however, considered that how the 'mixing' of abilities was achieved did not really matter, and that it was unnecessary 'to go to a lot of trouble to ensure an accurate spread'. Others were optimistic as to the outcome of their practices: 'We are rough and ready – deliberately so. *We arrange it so that the classes are balanced.*' A note of despair at ever achieving 'balance' was struck by others, based frequently on their perception of the difficulty of accounting adequately for factors such as personality and motivation; 'However careful we are' commented one head, 'groups become unbalanced and coalesce into something different', but added that 'in talking of mixed ability grouping we are talking about the ability of children to be educated together – not something *systematic*'. One school faced a peculiar problem in that a relatively high proportion of its pupils came from families in the services, and pupil transfer quickly altered a group's composition.

It was noted earlier than one reason for schools adopting mixed ability groups in the first year at least, was that they felt they had insufficient information from primary schools to be able to allocate pupils to streams. A number of problems were raised concerning transfer records. First, in some areas there was no common format for primary records, so that secondary schools receiving pupils from a number of feeders received information on a variety of skills and/or personal attributes, presented in different ways. Second, there was criticism of the content of the records, generally centred on lack of detail; and third, there was the criticism that the records were inadequately completed, with one head noting that personal rather than academic information was most frequently skimped. Among the schools studied, five in fact made no use of primary records in their allocation procedures, except for the identification of pupils in need of special tuition. In one of these, pupils were placed in classes on a geographical basis, with children from each village area being kept together in the same class, a practice which was seen as generally producing reasonably balanced groups. In another, where the records from the four feeder primaries were so diverse as to make systematic interpretation impossible, taking the form of examples of work, test scores and teacher ratings, discussions were held with the heads of the contributing schools; 'stars' were identified, as were children with reading problems. The latter were extracted to a remedial class, whilst the stars were allocated across forms. The other three schools which made no use of primary records described their allocation procedures as 'random', and in two, this was elaborated to 'random through the alphabet'. In one of these schools it was reported that the ability balance between forms varied considerably but that the school was 'not selecting for *mixed ability teaching*, but to teach children in houses'. It should be emphasized that in all these schools, though primary records were not used except in some instances to assist in the identification of children for withdrawal, there was nonetheless liaison with the feeder schools in the matter of grouping, through visits by specified staff to the feeder schools, or through a standing secondary-primary liaison group. In all, about one-third of the schools visited specifically mentioned discussions with primary colleagues on the allocation of children to groups.

For most schools, the primary record did, however, provide the material from which decisions concerning groupings were made. Three ways of utilizing primary records, dependent to a large extent on their content, were discernible. In the first, the primary record contained an overall global assessment in terms of a grade (usually on a five-point scale) and this was the main unit of information governing the sorting of children into groups of mixed ability. Five schools used such global assessments for this purpose. One head confessed that he did not know how primary heads interpreted such ratings, but that for the purposes of allocation within his secondary school 'they seemed to work'. We were not present at the actual time of allocation and it was difficult to ascertain the exact procedures applied to divide pupils graded A, B, C, D and E into forms with 'similar characteristics'. As stated earlier, it was clear that a number of heads considered that, having decided that the school policy was to have mixed ability groups, they could safely leave details of execution to their staff. This was particularly apparent in one school where ratings were received in a variety of forms from eight feeder schools.

Here, allocation of pupils to groups was the task of the head of lower school, a task performed 'in secrecy'. Some of the primaries contributing to the school used a three-point rating, others a five-point scale; a few gave no measure of attainment at all. The task was seen as using what information existed to classify all children as A, B or C; ratings had to be moderated in the light of many years' experience – the experience that a 'D from St. Luke's was equal to a B from St. Martin's', and that a certain kind of comment from St. Margaret's meant that a child should be classified as A. This task performed, 11 groups of equivalent 'ability' were constructed, but the methods were not always successful; on one occasion one form was so different that it (and, therefore, other groups) had to be 're-sorted'.

Whilst in the examples above schools wholly or partially relied on an overall rating or comment from the primary schools, the largest number of schools derived a classification of children from a single test score on the record card, or, rarely, used scores from different tests combined. Where a single test was used, this was a test of either verbal reasoning or reading age. Children might be listed in columns, for example, according to whether their VRQ scores were 130+, 120+, 110+, etc., and the teaching groups structured so that they had an equal number of children from each column. Some schools, however, disclaimed such rigour; in one, children were classified in five categories 'by intuition' using 'one or other of the test scores – usually communication skills'. Where more than one test was used to reach a classification – a practice found in only two schools – the tests concerned were reading, mathematics, verbal and non-verbal reasoning. In the one school where it was possible to ascertain how the scores were treated, a procedure of simply adding the scores together and classifying pupils in one of seven categories was adopted. Such a procedure, it will be noted, cannot take account of the variation of a pupil's performance over the tests; two pupils with a very different test profile, might achieve the same combined score.

The allocation procedures described above were in many cases modified to take account of other factors. Commonly, where there were house systems, schools tried to ensure that brothers and sisters were placed in the same house; several used information from the primary schools to attempt to keep friends together where possible. Others mentioned that they made sure that there were some children from each contributing school in each form. This was in some cases to ensure that all children would be in classes where they knew at least some of their companions, but in other schools it was also intended to help to lessen differences arising from the variety of contributory feeders, which might differ considerably in standards and in ethos. A conflict was perceived by one head between keeping children with their friends and achieving a fair social mix. 'Our primary colleagues', he reported, 'in endeavouring to maintain friendships have produced imbalance socially. One first year class has already got a reputation because too much attention was paid to the recommendations of primary teachers.' He added that 'We tend to get bogged down in VRQ and ignore social mix'. Relatively few heads mentioned this; where reference was made to 'social' factors, in most cases it was in the context of behaviour – the separation of known troublemakers: 'We try to see that there are not more than two rogues in any tutor group.'

Two schools mentioned specific problems that had arisen from allowing in one case the children, and in the other, parents, to contribute directly to the allocation procedure. In the first school, children had been asked to name four companions with whom they would like to be placed in teaching groups, which had produced results described as 'disastrous' in terms of the squabbling engendered and the difficulty of handling such information for a relatively large intake. The school had rapidly reverted to relying on the primary teachers' perceptions of friendship groups. In the second school, where a strong house system prevailed, parents had been asked to state their preference for their children's house, with the result that 'about ninety chose one house and three another'. These two examples clearly highlight the difficulties which can confront schools seeking to incorporate into their procedures an element of pupil or parent choice.

Other factors which determined allocation were the need in some inner-city schools to achieve a racial balance in forms, the desirability of having roughly equal numbers of boys and girls in a class, and, in two schools, the choice by pupils prior to entry of French or German as the foreign language to be studied in the first year. A further factor in one school was the special interests or abilities of children in music and sport, with children exhibiting excellence in these areas being distributed among the classes.

If the schools varied in the processes adopted for grouping children, there was one common element. Once the groups were formed, they generally remained the same, with the exception of the occasional transfer for behavioural reasons. Two schools mentioned a further reason for transfer – isolation. In one of these, which had a less stable population than other schools because of its high proportion of children from service families, a special attempt was made to spot the lonely child who was failing to fit in with the group in which he was placed, and around half a dozen such isolates were moved to other groups each year. Another school went so far as to apply the techniques of sociometry to identify the friendless and adjust groups accordingly. Apart from a few cases, however, schools generally retained groups intact, even though many reported the phenomenon of imbalance, of one group being 'better' or 'worse' than another. One head, however, had experimented with 're-shuffling' and found that it didn't work – 'it destroys the good groups as well as the bad'.

2.   Catering for pupils with special needs

One of the most problematic issues for schools wishing to organize their teaching in mixed ability groups is the extent to which pupils with special needs can be incorporated in such groups without depriving them of the kind of help they need or jeopardizing the progress of other children. Even in the relatively small number of schools in this study, a variety of approaches to this problem is apparent and demonstrates its many facets. At the very simplest level, we can distinguish among schools which have separate remedial classes, those which operate a system of withdrawal, and those which offer a combination of these approaches. The first – the separate remedial class as the only means of providing for the less able – was relatively rare, occurring in only three schools. Eighteen schools operated a policy of withdrawing pupils from certain lessons, with no static remedial group, and three of these schools also had an extra teacher who 'injected' help in lessons as required. Eight schools had both special remedial classes and withdrawal groups. Distinctions between these kinds of provision, however, are far from clear-cut. In practice there may be little difference between a school where pupils are taught in a separate remedial group for most of the time but join children in other classes for physical education and craft, and a school where withdrawal can mean for some pupils being extracted from the mainstream group for as much as 80 per cent of the school timetable.

Examples of different kinds of provision for the less able are presented in Appendix B. Emerging from these brief descriptions of the practice in eight of the schools are a number of key issues relating to policy and provision for children with learning difficulties. Many of these issues are clearly pertinent in many secondary schools, regardless of the practices adopted for grouping pupils.

i. Diagnosis.   Earlier studies (e.g. Sampson and Pumfrey, 1970) have reported a wide variation in the processes of identifying children who require special help at secondary level and have also demonstrated that such processes are seldom systematic. In the schools in this study we encountered a complex array of procedures in which teachers' recommendations, primary records and a variety of tests, received differing degrees of use and weighting. Reading tests were the most commonly-applied diagnostic tool; sometimes secondary schools relied on their primary feeders to supply scores on these (as in Examples 2 and 3) and in other instances the secondary schools themselves undertook the testing of their new intakes. Example 7 is interesting in its use of two stages of testing, with pupils on entry being given a group reading test and those with a reading age of less than 9.8 years being given further tests of a diagnostic nature (e.g. The Standard Reading Test; Daniels, J. C. and Diack, H., 1972). Two schools (Examples 4 and 5) were unusual in placing all pupils in mixed ability groups for their first weeks of secondary education to allow time for settling and for the schools' own diagnoses of special needs to be made.

The level of reading competence below which pupils were deemed to require special help varied considerably; in Example 8, for instance, it was a reading age of 8.5 years, whilst in Examples 3 and 7 it was 9.0 years and 9.5 years respectively. Where, as in Example 1, each faculty identified pupils considered to need special provision, abilities and skills other than reading might also be taken into account.

In identifying children who were to receive some form of special help, the school in Example 1 distinguished between pupils with learning difficulties and those with emotional and behavioural problems, and offered a different form of support for the two groups. In contrast some of the schools (e.g. Examples 2 and 6) considered that learning, emotional and behavioural difficulties were frequently closely intertwined and taught pupils with any of these together in remedial classes, where a 'secure home base' could be provided.

ii. Curriculum.   Two areas of particular interest emerge from the accounts of practice presented; the first concerns the parts of the curriculum for which pupils are withdrawn from mainstream groups in schools which operate a withdrawal system, and the second, the nature of special provision in such schools. Three schools out of those cited in the appendix (Examples 2, 3 and 8) withdrew pupils from modern languages so that they could receive extra tuition in reading, and in one school, in reading and mathematics. In Example 5, pupils were extracted from English and mathematics for special help with these subjects. In Examples 1 and 4 the aim was that pupils in withdrawal groups should follow a curriculum as similar to their mainstream peers as possible. The school in Example 6 was unusual in withdrawing pupils from games, home economics and craft for extra tuition in reading.

It is apparent even from these few examples that there is no consensus concerning the kind of curriculum which should be offered to children with learning difficulties although special tuition in reading emerges as the key element in most instances. Those parts of the curriculum which are omitted or curtailed in order to make way for such tuition merit attention, and we have above instances of omission in the case of languages, and of reduction in the case of games, home economics and craft. Some years ago, Her Majesty's Inspectorate, reporting their findings of a survey of the arrangements made in 158 secondary schools in Education Survey 15 (DES, 1971), stressed that the needs of slow learners were both 'wider and different' from those of their peers and that a suitably devised curriculum might be expected to 'concentrate less on attempting to remedy the irremediable and more in providing opportunities for growth and fulfilment in those areas of the curriculum where greater achievements are possible ...'. Detailed study of the curriculum for such pupils was outside the scope of this project; it was however apparent that this is an area where closer investigation of policy and provision is required, and indeed such study is now currently being undertaken by the NFER.

iii. Integrating pupils with the mainstream. An important view which contrasts with that quoted in the preceding paragraph is that slow learners should follow a similar curriculum to the rest of their year group as this facilitates their eventual transfer to the mainstream and keeps curricular opportunities open. Reference is made in Example 3 to the problems of integrating pupils after one year's separation in remedial classes where the main component was a crash course in reading, whilst Example 2 furnishes evidence of the difficulty of ever getting some pupils back into the mainstream – eight per cent of its fourth year pupils were still in a separate remedial group. Attempts to avoid the effects of sudden total integration appear in Example 4 where pupils were introduced to the mainstream group gradually, subject by subject, although here problems still arose in integrating pupils in modern language groups. The school in Example 7 encountered few problems of integration largely because its policy of daily withdrawal for a relatively short period meant that pupils spent most of their time in mixed ability classes anyway. It should be noted, however, that comparatively few children in this school had serious difficulties, and the effectiveness of the provision might be different were greater numbers of pupils involved.

iv. The role and status of remedial staff. To date, schools have sought to cater for pupils with learning difficulties by extracting them for special help, for part or all of the timetable. In Example 8, a policy of partial withdrawal was supplemented by the practice of remedial specialists going into classrooms and giving extra support to pupils as required. This is a relatively new way of deploying remedial teachers and, together with the school's practice of allocating time for such teachers to spend with subject departments giving advice on resources and teaching strategies, indicates a change in the role of the remedial teacher and the nature of his relationship with his colleagues. Such a change may be particularly beneficial to teachers of mixed ability classes, especially those encountering lower ability children for the first time. It has been claimed that many secondary teachers are not able to 'turn intellectual somersaults to cope with slow learners' and need help from their colleagues with special experience and training in this sphere (Hinson, 1977). Such changes in role make necessary a closer examination of the status within schools of those teachers who specialize in teaching slow learners, their career structure and their training. Awareness of the need to reflect the importance of the remedial specialist's role in terms of remuneration and level of appointment is found in Example 2 where the head of the remedial department was appointed on the same scale of post as the head of English. There is also evidence, however (e.g. Examples 1 and 7), of the view that the responsibility for meeting the needs of less academically gifted children should be shared by a wide range of teachers.

In examining schools' practices for catering for pupils with special needs the emphasis in this section has been on those experiencing learning difficulties. Heads rarely reported any arrangements made within their schools for the *ablest* of their children, although like many of their staff (v Chapter Five) they were concerned lest such pupils 'lost out' in a mixed ability class. Of the schools cited in the examples in Appendix B, two had some measure of formalized strategy for providing something extra for the more able on a *school basis*; in Example 1, those identified as particularly able were allocated a tutor, whose task was to devise a programme of additional activities whilst, in Example 7, faculty heads kept records of those outstanding in their subject and there were junior and senior clubs intended to provide additional experiences and stimulation for them. In both instances, it should be noted, school provision for the ablest took the form of extracurricular activity.

Chapter Five

Advantages and Difficulties – The Teachers' View

The main concern of the current study was to explore the views of teachers on mixed ability grouping and this chapter examines their evaluations of the outcomes of such a method of organization. Teachers' perceptions of advantage for pupils and of advantage and difficulty for themselves were probed in individual interviews. Teachers were also invited to indicate areas of research into mixed ability teaching which would be of particular interest to them and their responses highlighted areas of special concern and frequently confirmed comments expressed elsewhere. Heads of departments were asked to identify advantages to their departments arising from an unstreamed organization and also to report any difficulties encountered by their departmental staff. Material from these three areas of questioning is discussed in the paragraphs which follow, first in terms of pupil and teacher advantages and then of pupil disadvantages and teacher difficulties. In both instances perceptions are related to factors which may be associated with them – training, length and nature of experience, degree of involvement in mixed ability teaching, type of classroom organization and geographical location.

1. The identification of advantages for pupils and teachers in a mixed ability class

Of the 403 teachers who were substantially involved with classes containing a wide range of ability, 92 per cent considered that their pupils derived some advantage from the method of grouping used. The proportion perceiving benefits for the teacher was somewhat smaller – 75 per cent. Almost one-fifth, while not perceiving mixed ability classes as advantageous to themselves, nevertheless iden-

65

tified advantages for their pupils. In contrast, teachers wholly or mainly concerned with streamed, setted or banded classes almost always perceived these methods of organization as of advantage to both pupil and teacher. Teachers involved in mixed ability classes, however, produced on average 50 per cent more items identifying advantages for the pupil.

Since only eight per cent of those involved with mixed ability classes failed to indicate advantages for the pupils in a mixed ability class this group is not susceptible to any very complex analysis; it is interesting to note, however, that two-thirds of them also failed to identify any advantages for the teacher.

The relationship between teacher perceptions of advantages to themselves and the length of their service is explored in Table 5.1; this indicates that there are two groups of teachers less likely than others to identify advantages, a group still in their first year of teaching and those who have been teaching for more than ten years. This last group also produced almost half the responses, indicating a lack of advantages for pupils in unstreamed classes. Such results highlight the potential problems associated with the introduction of mixed ability teaching to schools where the majority of teachers may come into this category, as in area one (v Chapter Three).

Table 5.1:   *Length of experience and the identification of advantages for the teacher in a mixed ability class*

	Length of teachers' experience			
	Less than 1 year	1–5 years	6–9 years	10 years or more
N	(39)	(131)	(91)	(121)
	%	%	%	%
Advantages identified	74	81	81	65
No advantages	26	19	19	35
Total	100	100	100	100

Non response 21
$x^2 = 11.54$ $p < .01$.

Teachers whose *initial* training had contained some element dealing with mixed ability teaching identified teacher advantages in this mode of organization more frequently than their colleagues whose training had lacked this (Table 5.2); in view of teachers' criticisms of initial training reported in Chapter Three this finding may appear surprising. Those teachers who had received initial training in mixed ability teaching, however, were in most cases the younger teachers and whether their more favourable attitudes towards mixed ability grouping were the outcome of training or simply a reflection of greater flexibility and receptiveness to new approaches is unclear. No significant differences were found between the perceptions of those who had attended in-service courses concerned with mixed ability teaching and those who had not.

Table 5.2: *The relationship between initial training containing some element dealing with mixed ability teaching and the identification of advantages for the teacher*

| | Nature of initial training | |
	with mixed ability content	without mixed ability content
N	(128)	(230)
	%	%
Some advantages for the teacher	83	71
No advantages for the teacher	17	29
Total	100	100

Non response 45
$x^2 = 5.27$ $p < .1$

A further factor associated with the identification of advantages was the nature of the teacher's experience in terms of the types of schools in which he had worked. Teachers whose experience included teaching within the selective sector (grammar schools and secondary modern schools) were under-represented, and teachers whose experience included previous work in comprehensive schools, over-represented among those identifying advantages. This might be interpreted as a reflection of deeply-rooted attitudes or it might be seen as indicating that prior contact with the full range of ability gives the teacher a more confident base for teaching mixed ability groups than does experience with a population selected by ability.

The total teaching load of staff (i.e. percentage of the school week spent in teaching) was not related to whether they perceived mixed ability teaching to have advantages but the extent of their involvement with mixed ability classes was, with higher involvement being associated with a greater tendency to cite advantages for the teacher. The association was not statistically significant, but should be considered in conjunction with the highly significant relationship between the amount of time teachers spent in mixed ability teaching and the degree to which they considered their subjects suitable for teaching to unstreamed groups (v Chapter Six). Staff whose mixed ability work included teaching pupils in the fourth and fifth years did not differ significantly in their perceptions from those concerned with unstreamed groups in the first three years only.

Another factor which was considered in exploring teachers' perceptions was the organizational procedures used in the classroom. The claimed 'very frequent' use of the different approaches is illustrated in Table 5.3. Team teaching, constrained in many schools by unsuitable buildings, was not at all widely used and the proportion of teachers making very frequent use of group work or individualized learning was never more than a minority. Altogether, 54 per cent of teachers concerned with mixed ability classes claimed very frequent use of whole class teaching. Those teachers identify-

Table 5.3:   *Teachers' description of the very frequent use of a classroom method and their identification of advantages for the teacher*

Method used	Advantages given	No advantages
N	(281)	(90)
	%	%
Individualized	24	14
Small groups	17	11
Large groups	3	2
Whole class teaching	52	72
Team teaching	4	1
Total	100	100

Non response 32
$x^2 = 11.90$ $p < .1$

ing advantages for themselves made significantly more use of alternatives to whole class teaching than those perceiving no such advantages. Further discussion of the place of whole class teaching in mixed ability classes is carried out in the context of subject content in Chapter Six.

Other influences which might affect teacher perceptions are those associated with institutional and regional variations.

In the schools in area five, for example, only two teachers felt that the system of mixed ability grouping did not proffer any advantages for their pupils. The area was one containing a mix of urban and rural schools not by any means without problems, but teachers there generally felt that they had been involved in taking the decision to introduce mixed ability grouping and indeed they continued to have considerable freedom of choice concerning the actual grouping procedures to be adopted within their classes (three of the schools are in fact featured in Chapter Three as examples of the consultative and pragmatic/experimental modes of introducing mixed ability teaching). Their comments concerning the reasons for adopting mixed ability groups suggested that comprehensive reorganization had provided them with the 'ideal opportunity to experiment', to build up 'a successful pattern of teaching', to promote 'socially acceptable behaviour patterns' and to offer 'fairness in the true comprehensive spirit'. These schools also had very high proportions of teachers perceiving teacher advantages (an average of 91 per cent) and were surpassed in this respect only by one school from area two with a long history of mixed ability teaching in which all of the teachers interviewed identified advantages for both pupils and teachers.

In six schools relatively high proportions of the staff interviewed considered that mixed ability grouping was absolutely without advantage to the pupils, but in only one did this proportion exceed 24 per cent. Two schools from area one were exceptional in that more than 50 per cent of the interviewed teachers felt that mixed ability grouping offered no teacher advantages. It has already been noted that in this area teachers of more than ten years' experience were much more highly represented than elsewhere, a factor already shown to be associated with teachers' perceptions of mixed ability grouping. In both schools, moreover, mixed ability groups had been introduced at the time of reorganization as part of a 'package deal', in which teachers had played no part and with which many had disagreed (v Chapter Three).

2.   The nature of advantages for the pupil and the teacher in a mixed ability class

For the purposes of the following discussion pupil advantages have been divided into two categories: those which were not specifically related by teachers to any particular group of pupils (Table 5.4) and those which teachers reported as being particularly associated with pupils of a certain ability (Table 5.6). Advantages for the teacher are listed in Table 5.5. In the commentary which follows these will be considered where possible with associated pupil advantages.

It should be emphasized that many teachers concerned with mixed ability classes did not appear to see any real distinction between their own interests and those of their pupils and did not find it easy to analyse their experiences in terms of the implications for the pupil, the teacher and their subject specialisms; this difficulty can be readily understood in view of the complexity of the relationship and the interaction between various aspects of all three. Features of everyday life are seldom subjected to such analysis and a reaction from teachers was 'I have never thought about it in that way'.

Table 5.4:   *Advantages not related to any specific ability group for pupils in a mixed ability class as identified by the teacher*

Nature of pupil advantage	Percentage of teachers (N = 403)
Labelling avoided	36
Personal and social development fostered	33
Classroom climate improved	31
Improved motivation	22
Individual needs more effectively met	17
Improved behaviour	14
Improved attainment	13
Improved opportunities	12
'Real world' reflected	8
Transition to secondary school eased	6
General advantages	14
* (The same teacher may be included in more than one category.)	

Table 5.5: *Advantages for the teacher in a mixed ability cl identified by the teacher*

Nature of teacher advantage	Percentage of teachers (N = 403)
Work satisfaction increased	35
Behaviour problems decreased	29
Pupil-teacher interaction improved	28
Teaching skills developed	15
New interest in subject aroused	8
Labelling of teachers avoided	5
Teacher-teacher interaction improved	5

* (The same teacher may be included in more than one category.)

i. Advantages not related to a specific ability group

(a) Labelling avoided

The major advantage of mixed ability grouping for the pupil, mentioned by over a third of the teachers, was the avoidance of labelling, and in this the teachers' perceptions of the main benefit endorses the heads' most frequently given reason for its introduction (v Chapter Three). Teachers mentioned this advantage with reference to all pupils but especially to the able and the less able. For the able the avoidance of labelling prevented the 'creating of top dogs as in a streamed class'; for the less able it meant giving a chance to those who 'in the low streams felt second class', avoiding the 'self-fulfilling prophecy' that results from 'giving to those that have and denying to those that have not'. The avoidance of labelling in a mixed ability class appeared also as a widening of opportunity – 'they have all got an equal chance', and was seen as improving the pupils' whole motivation and self-evaluation – avoiding that dreadful sense of failure right up to the fifth year'. It was interesting to note however how frequently teachers who condemned labelling went on to talk of their pupils in terms of those that were 'less able', 'more able' and 'average', implying that these were recognizable and discrete groups within their classrooms, and indeed because of the nature of teacher responses in this respect many of our analyses are in terms of such distinctions.

A small number of teachers, five per cent of those substantially involved with mixed ability groups, saw the avoidance of labelling as having advantages for themselves, pointing out that without 'bottom' classes you avoid 'bottom' teachers, and a number of heads of department noted an improvement in teacher morale and general attitudes as a departmental advantage arising from the introduction of mixed ability grouping. This had obviously removed for some teachers the feeling that they were considered within their school to be inferior, as well as providing for them the opportunity of meeting a full range of ability. Their view was confirmed by a similar proportion of those teachers who worked wholly or mainly with ability selected groups, who recorded dissatisfaction with the labelling to which they as teachers were subjected. Awareness of the labelling hazard for pupils was also highly pronounced among the teachers of such groups, almost half of whom identified it as the major disadvantage for their pupils, with effects spreading far beyond the classroom. Typical comments included, 'they feel isolated from the rest of the school who call them "dummies"'; 'the whole set up is disruption-oriented like a penal unit'; 'they always lose out'. One teacher encapsulated his views of the long-term effects of labelling the less able with the comment: 'One day they will have to leave the group – but it is generally to join other hewers of wood and drawers of water.'

(b)   Personal and social development
The pupil advantage identified by the second largest number of teachers, 33 per cent of the sample, was concerned with the fostering of pupils' personal and social development within a mixed ability class. Some teachers' comments in this area provided an illuminating picture not only of what they saw as advantages for their pupils, but also of the aspects of personal and social development which they valued most highly. Certain key threads were discernable in the perceptions of many of the teachers. The first of these was an approval for the stability of the social unit in which mixed ability teaching takes place. This was said to give the pupil 'added security and confidence' and to 'encourage self-sufficiency and a sense of individual responsibility'. Other teachers recorded that 'all getting on well together, respecting each other's individual differences and each other's work' led to an increase in tolerance of individual foibles within the group. Another important aspect of this perception was the 'ironing out of anomalies of background', social class differences being specifically mentioned by many teachers.

Although 'social' advantages were often claimed within a mixed ability organization, however, the nature of such advantages was frequently not articulated. The phrase 'the usual social advantages' was employed by many teachers in their interview and this unquestioning expression of social benefits was reflected in an almost total lack of interest in exploring the social outcomes of mixed ability teaching in the subsequent group discussions. Because of this, the precise nature of such advantages and the criteria used by teachers to determine the social environment of the classroom remain ill-defined.

The emphasis teachers gave to the personal and social development of pupils appeared to be associated in some degree with their previous experience. Teachers recording the fostering of personal and social development of their pupils as an advantage represent 28 per cent of the teachers with no other experience, 33 per cent of those whose experience excluded mixed ability teaching and 38 per cent of those with mixed ability experience. Teachers whose previous teaching had included experience in the comprehensive system tended to mention this advantage more frequently than their colleagues without such experience. None of those 76 teachers wholly or mainly concerned with ability-selected groups mentioned factors within their classrooms contributing towards the personal and social development of their pupils and some (12) perceived their grouping system to be 'socially divisive'. The view expressed here was that social divisions were replicated within the various streams and pupils were 'not made aware of each other's difficulties and differences'. A history teacher added the further comment that 'the really bright children become quite phobic; they are terrified of demotion and the less able develop a deprivation complex'.

(c) 'Classroom climate'
The third most common perception in the area of pupil advantage concerned what might be termed 'classroom climate'. Thirty-one per cent of the sample considered that mixed ability classes provided a happy working atmosphere in which co-operation was fostered and that this provided very real advantages for the pupil. Factors already mentioned in the preceding paragraphs contributed to such an atmosphere – pupils' feelings of security, of not being pre-judged and of respect for those of different talents, achievements and backgrounds.

Many teachers who reported an improvement in classroom at-

mosphere as an advantage for their pupils also cited an improvement in pupil-teacher interaction as a benefit for themselves. A
teacher of religious education in a large urban school with a
ten-year tradition of mixed ability teaching noted, for example, that
'pupils in a mixed ability class don't seem to be rejecting each other,
the teacher or the work in any way'. Other teachers considered that
they had become more aware of pupils as individuals – an enticing
comment here from one teacher was that 'I grew up and expanded
as a teacher because I was thrust into talking to children face to face
rather than as a class'. Teachers also reported that the increased
co-operation among pupils constituted a teacher advantage because
the teacher 'could get a bit of support from the class'.

(d)   Motivation

The view that a mixed ability class offered motivational advantages
for all the pupils was recorded by over a fifth of the teachers. The
pupils were described as 'working harder', 'showing greater all
round interest', not having such 'limited expectations of themselves', and even those who would not normally evince much
enthusiasm for work were reported by these teachers as being
'inspired by those who are interested'.

(e)   Individual needs more effectively met

Another advantage for the pupils in mixed ability classes, mentioned by 17 per cent of the sample, concerned meeting their
individual learning needs. This factor appeared to be associated
with teaching methodology and was often related to the opportunities offered through individualized resource-based learning. As
a group those who cited the meeting of individual needs as an
advantage of a mixed ability approach claimed to make much more
frequent use of individualized work and small groups than their
colleagues. Three comments capture the essence of the advantage
as seen by teachers: 'They are doing what they want to as individuals'; 'Pupils can work at their own pace and it is easier to find
out an individual's problem areas'; and 'The pupil has a wide range
of acceptable achievements to choose from'.

   Although a similar proportion of teachers wholly or mainly
concerned with ability-selected groups claimed a similar advantage
for their classes, their comments tended to emphasize the tailoring

of materials to a whole class, e.g. 'the work is nearer to their own pace'; 'there are fewer gaps between ability and the work demanded'. Eleven teachers of such classes considered their mode of selective organization advantageous in terms of meeting individual needs since it avoided accentuating individual differences. One of these teachers, a linguist, with over ten years' experience, stressed the value for the individual of 'knowing where you are going with people of the same academic and social outlook'.

(f) Behaviour

The 'grouping of children by ability with the concomitant narrowing of language facility and range of social origin' was seen by some of those interviewed as leading inevitably to 'sump' or 'sink' groups, in which were concentrated all the disruptive elements within the school as well as those genuinely in need of intensive training in basic skills. The avoidance of this situation and the subsequent improvement in pupil behaviour was identified by 14 per cent of the teachers as a pupil advantage associated with mixed ability grouping, whilst 29 per cent identified the reduction of behaviour problems as an advantage for those teaching mixed ability groups. For these teachers such groups meant the avoidance of the situation where 'one receives a whole class of children who are anti-school' and offered them the possibility, 'when not faced by a class with a reputation, of being able to behave in a more reasonable way'. The 'dilution of disruption' ensured that the teacher was 'not put into so many confrontation situations'. A head of mathematics in a large urban school noted pragmatically: 'We do not have enough teachers who can keep order – unstreamed classes overcome this.' Altogether, over a third (34 per cent) of the teachers interviewed recorded improved behaviour as an advantage of mixed ability grouping for the pupil, the teacher, or both. Not surprisingly, this perception was rare among probationers but otherwise appeared independent of length of service, teachers with more than ten years' service being fully represented.

The perception of disciplinary difficulties in lower sets was confirmed by 21 per cent of the teachers wholly or mainly concerned with such classes. Teachers talked of the problems of trying to motivate those of lower ability and the discipline problems which arose when 'all the deprived children are together'.

(d)   Attainment

Fifty-two teachers who were substantially involved with mixed ability groups recorded an improvement in the attainment of all pupils in their classes, and this was seen to include an improvement in both the quantity and the quality of the work done. Concerning quality, the comments referred to the 'widened range of pupil contributions', the 'quality of discussion', and the 'more questioning attitude' adopted by the pupils. Favourable comparisons with the comparable age range in a grammar school were made by a head of English department, with lengthy service in an urban grammar school. He talked of the reduction in the gap between the different levels of ability, achieved by a 'levelling up rather than a levelling down process'.

(h)   Opportunity

Almost as many teachers felt that the 'chance of success' offered by the 'more open-ended goals' and the 'access to a wide range of resources' improved opportunities for all pupils within a mixed ability class. Emphasis was also placed on the provision of 'equal opportunity for all' and on 'leaving options open', teachers' comments in many cases being similar to those classified under the avoidance of labelling (2.i.a.).

(i)   Real world

Some teachers (32) accorded to the mixed ability class the particular advantage for the pupil that it represented a reflection of the real world. The fact that each class contained a cross-section was seen as of great value 'enriching discussion by the interchange of news and views between children of different backgrounds'. This 'cross-fertilization' was valued for the 'concrete example' it provided of what these teachers considered to be the philosophy of the real world – 'showing that each person has something to offer'.

(j)   Transition to secondary school eased

Considering the views of teachers and head teachers concerning the variable standard of junior school records (v Chapter Four) the facilitation of transfer by using mixed ability grouping was mentioned with surprising infrequency. Only six per cent of the teachers identified the easing of transition as a pupil advantage, and it was made explicit by some that this was seen in terms of a short diagnostic period – 'all the better to set you by!' Other teachers mentioned the advantages of 'settling in' with primary school friends thus avoiding much of the risk of the 'shock of change'.

(k)   'General' advantages

A substantial number of teachers (56) made comments not readily classifiable into any one of the above categories, but which suggested that they considered mixed ability classes to provide a generally more advantageous environment for students. Their comments included those which emphasized the negative aspects of streaming and the view that 'any selection procedure produces a lot of mistakes'.

ii.   *Advantages related to pupils within a specific range of ability*

Many of the comments recorded related to pupils of a specified ability, and indeed these outnumbered those not tied to a particular level of ability by 3:2. The percentage of teachers specifying advantages for pupils of different abilities is shown in Table 5.6.

(a)   The less able

Altogether, almost half the teachers substantially concerned with mixed ability classes identified advantages of some kind for the less able students, and this perception was not found to be associated with their previous experience. The advantage given by the greatest number of teachers concerned an improvement in the motivation of these pupils. Twenty three per cent of teachers produced responses which could be included in this category, and their comments indicated that several factors were involved in the motivation of the less able; some recorded that 'the less able responded well to being in a fairly industrious working atmosphere', others that they were 'stimulated to achieve better results by seeing the work of the more able', and some teachers noted that 'because children responded more readily to each other's suggestions the less able were directly helped by the presence of pupils with more ability'. While the less able were seen as gaining in confidence, many teachers specified that this was not achieved by a loss of realism; indeed it was said that pupils gained 'a fair indication of their own abilities in relation to those of others in their group without any building up of a sense of failure'. Other teachers considered more directly the implications for learning: 'The pupils believe in themselves. They are carried on by their positive attitudes and behaviour where before they would have given up.'

Table 5.6:   *Teachers citing advantages related to pupils within a specific range of ability*

Nature of Pupil Advantage	Percentage of Teachers Citing Advantage (N = 403)		
	More Able %	Middle Range %	Less Able %
Motivation improved	1	5	23
Attainment improved	3	3	11
Opportunity improved	2	2	11
Generally advantageous	5	3	11

* (The same teacher may be included in more than one category.)

Three other aspects of advantage for the less able – improved attainment, improved opportunities and general advantages – were each commented on by 11 per cent of the teachers. With regard to attainment, the mixed ability group was seen as bringing about an upgrading of the standards of work of the less able 'towards the mean' resulting from the happier atmosphere, the opportunity to work with their more able fellows and the competition that such a partnership produced. The teacher's view of acceptable outcomes appeared to be an important factor in how he perceived the less able pupil's attainments in a mixed ability group. A modern languages teacher from a large urban school which had been involved in mixed ability teaching for some six years illustrates this point in his comment 'All are able to achieve success *at some level.*'

Teachers claiming increased opportunities for the less able pupils tended to emphasize the removal of restrictions for such pupils in terms of material resources – 'it is no longer a case of the less able getting the least interesting materials' – and the increase in the range of activities and teachers that were encountered. Advantages classified as 'general' included those concerned with the avoidance of peer group and institutional discrimination, exemplified by the comment of a geography teacher in a small community-based rural school: 'it avoids the less able pupils feeling that they are less important or socially of less value'.

(b)   Pupils of average and above average ability
Advantages specifically for the more able pupils within a mixed ability class were mentioned by relatively few teachers with the largest group of responses, made by five per cent of the sample, falling in to a general area dealing with factors such as the opportunity offered for extra responsibilities within such a class and the insight and team spirit fostered by being involved in helping their less able peers. Three per cent of the sample felt that if materials were adequately prepared the really able could 'work independently and become more resourceful' and would be fully stretched by being able to pursue a topic further than in a streamed class. A similar proportion of teachers identified motivational benefits for the more able and talked in terms of 'better attitudes' extending into the years following a mixed ability basic course.

Few teachers also talked of pupils in the middle range of ability gaining from the experience of mixed ability grouping. Five per cent described the 'inspiration offered by the contact with their more able peers' and a smaller proportion mentioned an improvement in attainment. The number of teachers considering that opportunities for this 'middle majority' were improved was even smaller. A teacher of English with five years of mixed ability experience made an interesting observation as regards the concentration by many teachers on the extremes of ability and the detrimental effect this might have on the majority of pupils who were thereby overlooked. The majority of pupils in the class, he noted, seldom seemed the subject of enquiry, their position all too often being accepted as 'an unquestioned fact of school life'.

iii.   Other advantages for teachers
Certain of the perceptions held by teachers concerning advantages for themselves have already been considered. Those listed in Table 5.5 and as yet undiscussed will now be described.

(a)   Work satisfaction
The most commonly held perception of advantage for the teacher, mentioned by over one third of those substantially involved with

mixed ability groups was an increased satisfaction with their work. Whilst a number of teachers commented that the 'more relaxed', 'much calmer', 'much more natural atmosphere' provided a 'more satisfying and less wearing' environment for the teacher, an important factor associated with work satisfaction appeared to be the effort required to achieve successful outcomes from a mixed ability class. This was epitomized by the comment from a young English teacher in a large multiracial school who said: 'You have to pull out all the stops; it involves much more effort but it produces better teaching. It can bring out the best in every teacher.' Many teachers talked in similar terms of their responses to the challenge; frequent reference was made to the 'stimulating effect on one's performance as a teacher', the 'change of role from director to guide', the 'more exciting teaching methods' that could be introduced and 'the unpredictability and challenge' offered by the diversity of talent within each group. The opportunities mixed ability groups afforded were grouped by ability, and indeed a number of the teachers problems' encountered in lower streams of schools where pupils were grouped by ability, and indeed about one in ten of the teachers of streamed or setted classes reported a lack of work satisfaction, the most usual contributing factor being involvement in teaching 'lower sets', which produced such comments as: 'Depressing – even though you try not to let your expectations come through'; 'It is hard to feel achievement'. Another teacher commented, perhaps surprisingly, on the general *lack* of challenge: 'It is so very undemanding, no organization or imagination is required and therefore you get much less imaginative teachers.' Where teachers concerned with streamed or setted classes did record a satisfaction with their work, their comments generally emphasized academic progress.

(b)   Skills and interest

The development of teaching skills was considered as a teacher advantage by 60 of the teachers substantially involved with mixed ability classes. The general tone of their comments suggested that the method of organization avoided 'the pitfall of complacency' and offered a situation in which 'the teacher can discover things about himself – ideas, preconceptions, insights'. Thirty-three of the teachers interviewed recorded a new interest in their subject area arising from their perceived need to look again at what was being taught and how. This perspective was put most succinctly by a geography teacher from a large urban comprehensive school with a multiracial intake: 'Unstreaming made us rethink the whole meaning of our subject and our educational philosophy and look critically at our resources.'

(c)   Teacher-teacher interaction
Mixed ability teaching was seen as bringing down the barriers between teachers by a small group (five per cent) who talked about the 'oppenness of the new situation' and the need for 'preparation not to be an enormous burden but a shared exercise'. With co-operation came a sharing of problems and techniques resulting in a reduction in the isolation of the individual teacher, and a number of heads of department reported that the more intensive discussion of content and method produced in their colleagues a new awareness of both the nature of the subject and the needs of pupils.

3.   The identification of disadvantages for the pupil and difficulties for the teacher in a mixed ability class

It was apparent, in isolating features which teachers perceive as disadvantages for their pupils and as offering difficulties for themselves, that what was seen as an advantage by one teacher might be perceived by a colleague as a disadvantage or a difficulty. For example, one feature that emerged early in the project was a perception of the uncertainty of outcomes in a mixed ability group. Whereas some teachers talked in terms of this being 'exciting', 'challenging', 'stimulating', 'bringing about a new dynamism' – i.e. contributing essentially to what was later identified as an increase in work satisfaction – others identified this same aspect as 'threatening', 'inhibiting the role of the teacher' and 'contributing to the overall stress of teaching'. It became clear that such varying interpretations could not be fully explored in terms of variables such as the nature and length of previous experience, but needed to be related to individual personality, attitudes and values. Even if satisfactory measures of these factors could be found, however, such an exercise lay outside the limits of the project's resources.

The proportions of teachers specifying disadvantages for pupils and difficulties for themselves were very similar; only 39 (ten per cent) teachers suggested that mixed ability teaching had no disadvantages for the pupils and only 31 (eight per cent) recorded no difficulties for themselves. No evidence was found of an association between the identification of adverse factors within the mixed ability class and the nature of previous experience, overall teaching load and mixed ability teaching load (i.e. percentage of total teaching time spent with mixed ability classes). Neither regional nor institutional factors appeared associated with differences in perception, nor was any association found between the use or non-use of alternative teaching methods and a teacher's perception of disadvantage or difficulty.

4.   The nature of disadvantages for the pupil and difficulties for the teacher

Over two thirds of teachers' comments concerning disadvantages for pupils in a mixed ability class were made with reference to pupils of a particular ability (Table 5.7), with disadvantages for the more able students being mentioned most frequently (5 per cent of teachers). Disadvantages for the less able were reported by 45 per cent of teachers, but, as in the area of advantages, few teachers (seven per cent) referred to those in the middle range of ability. Thirty per cent of the comments were unrelated to ability and included those which described reduced motivation, lowered attainment and restricted opportunities for all pupils in a mixed ability class.

In the paragraphs which follow we consider first comments made with reference to pupils at the extremes of the ability range and then examine other factors which teachers cited as difficulties arising in a mixed ability setting together with institutional constraints which exacerbated them.

i.   Disadvantages and difficulties at the extremes of the ability range

(a)   The more able

Teachers' comments focussed extensively on the attainment of the more able in mixed ability classes and reflected concern over a lack of 'academic texture' and the view that in such classes able children would not be extended. Teachers suggested that without the stimulation of an able peer group 'the faster ones soon slow down' and the outcome was that 'the most able sink to a happy mean' and soon 'learn to accept a lower standard of work'. The problem of reduced motivation for abler pupils in a mixed ability class was implicit in many teachers' comments concerning the attainment of these pupils and was made explicit in the remarks of 46 teachers. These teachers identified as inhibiting motivation, frustration at 'not being stretched', and at 'not getting attention'; 'boredom' resulting from 'waiting for the slower ones' and 'resentment' at being asked to extend themselves when they were doing better than the rest anyway. A further factor which was considered as contributing towards a reduction of the motivation of the more able was the ease with which such pupils could 'switch off' without this coming to the attention of the teacher.

Table 5.7: *Teachers citing disadvantages for pupils of differing abilities in a mixed ability class*

Ability of pupil	% Teachers* N = 403	% Items N = 750
Disadvantages for:		
Less able	45	27
Average	7	4
More able	59	39
All pupils (i.e. Comments unrelated to ability)	53	30
Total		100

*(The same teacher may be included in more than one category)

One teacher noted that 'they are more neglected than held back' and a number of teachers described the situation where the able 'are forced to sit when they know the answers – they give up bothering to put their hands up'. Many teachers suggested that this was the effect of 'teaching to the middle', and the problem of 'where to pitch the lesson' was one frequently raised in discussions with the research team and implied an attempt to treat the mixed ability class as an homegeneous group. Further, a teacher of history from a school long used to mixed ability teaching was not alone in suggesting that a reduction in attainment was not uncommon 'if the teacher is unskilled or uncommitted – the problem is one of the two extremes being ignored'. He went on to add that 'this is a problem of streaming too but it is just not admitted'.

Some teachers suggested that problems resulted from the difficulty in identifying the more able and these were exacerbated in a mixed ability class since such pupils can 'often be carried as a passenger, not working to capacity, in a class where you expect a wide range of attainment'. Even where able pupils were identified solutions were not always readily available: 'It is not possible to stretch the top person without close attention and without the guidance of the teacher.' The allocation of extension exercises could, in the opinion of some teachers, reduce drive unless they were carefully introduced. More than a third of the teachers wholly or mainly concerned with streamed classes, in contrast, considered that such a grouping permitted the opportunity of 'putting more pressure on the able to achieve', due to the 'extra work' that such a group could be offered.

As already noted, many of the comments describing mixed ability teaching reveal an explicit or implicit assumption of work geared to the middle of the ability range. A reduction of opportunities for the more able was also seen, however, to arise from the teacher's preoccupation with the less able, exemplified by the teacher of religious education who said 'the brighter ones have to get by on their own as the teacher has to give two-thirds of his attention to the less able'. A number of teachers referred to 'general disadvantages' for the more able and produced statements concerning the bright being 'penalized', 'getting disheartened', 'suffering' and needing to be constantly reminded that they will soon be 'competing against pupils of the same ability'. Many of the comments made by teachers indicated that they had established largely cognitive goals for their more able pupils whereas for other pupils different goals, associated with control and integration, were emphasized.

Concerning teachers' difficulties, a number of heads of department reported that their staff had raised problems relating to meeting the needs of more able pupils (Table 5.1A), and indeed about a fifth of those teachers substantially involved with mixed ability classes spoke of the difficulties presented to the teacher in meeting these pupils' needs; it is almost certain, however, that many more teachers felt that they had already implied teacher difficulties in their comments relating to disadvantages for the pupil. The only new aspect to emerge from comments on problems for the teacher concerned meeting the requirements of external examinations. A head of mathematics department, for example, most of whose experience had been in a grammar school, expressed anxiety over delay in specialization – 'O-level students do not have time to adjust; there should be setting for three or four years before the examination.' Over 30 teachers suggested the exploration of ways of catering for the more able in mixed ability groups as an area where research was needed (Table 5.2A).

The citing of disadvantages for the more able did not appear to be associated with teachers' previous experience, either in terms of length of service or the type of institution in which they had served; a very highly significant association was found, however, with teachers' perceptions of the suitability of their subject for mixed ability work (Table 5.3A). As might be expected, those who considered their discipline appropriate for mixed ability work were far less likely to refer to disadvantages for the abler pupil.

(b)   The less able

Altogether, 45 per cent of teachers identified disadvantages for the less able pupil in a class comprising a wide range of ability. Over a third made comments which were grouped as generally disadvantageous, and many of these again drew attention to the problems which arose when teachers 'aimed for the middle'. A head of science department, for example, claimed that 'the less able miss out because the teacher pitches for an average level', a view confirmed by the head of the English department in a large urban comprehensive who commented that 'whatever the theory, in practice one ends up teaching to the middle'. Many other teachers considered that time constraints inhibited the provision of the individual attention needed by those lacking in the basic skills of literacy and numeracy. The effects on the less able were described as 'soul destroying' due to their 'feelings of inadequacy'. Many teachers pointed out that the brisk pace necessary to ensure the continued interest of the majority resulted in the less able 'soon being left behind'. It was noted that they tended to sit together and faced considerable problems because 'they cannot read or understand the material on the workcards'. *A reduction* in the motivation of the less able in mixed ability groups was specifically mentioned by a number of teachers (cf. p.77).

Almost a quarter of those substantially involved with mixed ability classes associated their difficulties in teaching such groups with meeting the needs of the less able. A head of science in a school with a long tradition of mixed ability teaching pointed out that 'the majority of staff are lacking in the ability or knowledge to teach basic skills'. Other teachers stressed the necessity of ensuring that work card language was comprehensible to those with low reading ages. The integration of those coming from remedial groups presented problems for some teachers, and where the school operated a withdrawal policy the number of necessary co-ordinations could present difficulties. Identification of the less able within a group of wide ability was also recorded as a difficulty; the head of a science department, for example, reported his experience that 'the less able can often get along by copying and their lack of ability may not be recognized until much later on'.

A number of those teachers wholly or mainly concerned with teaching ability-selected groups commented on the problems of teaching less able children in classes where pupils' ability was wide-ranging. An experienced remedial teacher stressed that segregation, whilst in many respects reprehensible, 'did cater for the less able academically' and pointed out that in many mixed ability classes 'teachers are often unwilling and unable to do this'. Another, an English specialist, drew attention to the difficulties which arose when lack of academic achievement was accompanied by social immaturity. In such cases children could not cope in a large class and were rejected by groups of their fellow pupils in a mixed ability class.

The problems raised within subject departments as reported by departmental heads (Table 5.1A) most commonly related to difficulties associated with the least academically motivated and those of low academic attainment. Many departmental heads were concerned that their staff lacked the expertise to deal with problems associated with an inadequacy in literacy and numeracy skills. A smaller number, however, expressed the opinion that subject specialist teachers were most usefully occupied in teaching their specialism rather than in attempting to remedy such deficits.

ii.   Other difficulties associated with mixed ability grouping

Whilst problems relating to the most and least able pupils dominated the teachers' comments, a number of other difficulties were also reported by substantial numbers of teachers. These are classified in Table 5.8 in two groups; those associated with classroom teaching and those arising from what we have termed 'institutional factors' such as class size, design of buildings and insufficient or inadequate equipment.

(a)   Difficulties related to classroom teaching

i.   Meeting pupil needs, pacing work and assessment
Concern over 'meeting pupil needs' – a concern not related to any particular level of ability – headed the list of items relating to teacher difficulties and contained responses from 39 per cent of teachers (Table 5.8). Exploration of what teachers meant when

Table 5.8:   *Teachers' perceptions of difficulties in teaching mixed ability classes*

Nature of difficulty	Percentage of teachers* N = 403
(a) *Difficulties related to classroom teaching*	
Meeting pupil needs (no ability group specified)	39
Increased preparation/marking	32
Increased need for resources	24
Demands on teacher expertise	18
Teacher stress/role uncertainty	14
Pacing work	11
Assessment	10
Classroom control	8
Teaching subject-related skills†	6
(b) *Difficulties related to institutional factors*	
Class size too large	20
Design/deployment of buildings	17
Length of lesson unit	5
Timetable constraints	5
Insufficient money/equipment	5

*(The same teacher may be included in more than one category)
†(These are explored in Chapter Six)

they talked of such concern indicated two interacting factors as contributing to their anxiety in this respect; both reflected teachers' perceptions of their role within the classroom. The first of the factors was the pressure placed upon the teacher when he represented the only mediating agent in the classroom: 'You tend to get swamped'; 'Only one pair of hands – you cannot get around to everyone'; 'The teacher is called on to turn all ways at once'. A teacher of modern languages in a school where the mixed ability organization extended up to the end of the second year (i.e. pupils of 13-plus) pinpointed the particular difficulty faced by modern linguists where 'the biggest resource is the teacher and you just cannot spread yourself six ways'. The other factor was a consequence of a whole class methodology and was the problem of trying to 'provide for all while teaching to the middle'. In the words of one teacher: 'The tendency is not to see the pupils as members of a mixed ability class but to teach them as you would any other class.' Where resource-based learning was used some teachers recorded that the difficulty remained: 'I still tend to gear essential work to the middle although I do make use of a system of "starred questions".'

A closely-related problem reported by over 40 teachers was that of 'pacing' the work for a class of mixed ability, and the comments of these teachers confirm that whole class teaching was widely practised and was also perceived as unavoidable. A science teacher with more than six years teaching experience from a community college provides an example of this: 'They can't all keep up – the only way of trying to gain teacher satisfaction is by teaching them all as a group and moving more slowly.' This view was endorsed by the head of a technical studies department with more than ten years teaching experience, who said: 'You must class teach, you can't have 25 to 35 pupils all doing different work.' Of the teachers who identified difficulties arising from the pace of work only one in fact did not also report using whole class teaching very frequently. This method of organization was indeed very frequently used by the majority of teachers of mixed ability classes, although the extent of its use in lessons clearly varied; many teachers, for example, described teaching to the whole class for the introduction of new material and for concluding a sequence of work. Almost a fifth of the research suggestions from teachers showed that their prime concern was with classroom method and organization (Table 5.2A) and the evaluation of different teaching approaches, including whole class teaching, the use of groups and of various resources.

Pacing a pupil's work appropriately demands that adequate assessment be made of his progress. However, although a frequent subject for debate in teacher group meetings, only 40 teachers raised assessment as a teacher difficulty in their interviews. Problems centred on how to grade work in such a way as to maintain standards but avoid demotivating low achievers. Final assessments of pupils proceeding to bands, sets or streams also presented difficulties. A further problem arose in some schools where pupils who had in the early secondary years been assessed only in relation to their own previous effort and attainment were confronted with normative assessment in the fourth and fifth years.

ii. Resources, preparation and demands on teacher expertise
The preparation of resources was seen by many teachers as an integral part of mixed ability teaching. Requests to the project team for resources were common although where mixed ability teaching had been recently introduced, understanding of the concept was frequently limited to 'the worksheet'. In those areas where mixed ability groups had been operating for several years the availability of resources was not seen as so critical and a widening of the term to include a variety of mediating agents was much more common. Nearly a quarter of those substantially involved with mixed ability classes recorded an increased need for resources. However, whilst a link between resource-based learning and mixed ability teaching was acknowledged by many of the teachers interviewed, the use of a mediating agent other than the teacher gave rise to obvious concern, particularly among teachers with a traditional view of their role. A small number of teachers made clear their feelings of being displaced from their former central position in the learning situation. Many teachers pointed out that there was a severe lack of published material suitable for use with a wide range of abilities and, while this extended right across the curriculum, some areas appeared exceptionally difficult to resource from outside the school. Teachers stressed that, unless they were prepared to rely heavily on straightforward worksheets, preparation required 'immense thought and expertise'. Almost a fifth of the teachers expressed awareness of this increased need for expertise, picking out factors such as the skill and organizational ability needed both inside and outside the classroom.

Where and how to obtain such expertise became a theme of many teacher discussions. As reported in Chapter Three, initial training, even for those recently entering the profession, was frequently not seen as offering opportunities, nor those responsible for its organization as possible sources of help. Whilst criticisms of in-service courses was common, however, it was apparent in discussions with teacher groups that the demands made by some of the teachers were often somewhat unrealistic. It would not be too great a distortion to suggest that the demand to 'tell me what to do and how to do it' was typical of a number of groups. Many of the teachers were obviously 'imprisoned' within their classrooms and had not identified the expertise existing within their schools, sometimes not even that within their own department.

Meeting the lack of stimulus material for use with a mixed ability class gave rise to difficulties due both to the demands on teachers' time and to the need for expertise. Barriers to teacher co-operation and the sharing of resources seemed little diminished by a mixed ability organization, and the proclaimed 'ownership' of particularly effective teaching/learning resources was common. A senior teacher responsible for mathematics pointed out the difficulty he had found in obtaining the co-operation of staff to prepare or share resources. Many staff therefore undertook the preparation of resources in isolation and were, in effect, 'alone with a Banda'.

iii.   Teaching role

As the preceding discussion suggests, a rejection of any change in teaching role was not uncommon and 55 teachers made comments indicative of stress or uncertainty over the role demands of a mixed ability organization. Some questioned the lack of defined objectives and drew a contrast between 'the theory and the practice'. A mathematics teacher of more than 10 years experience working in a large suburban comprehensive school, recorded the stress created when 'you become an assistant or a servant rather than the dominant factor in the classroom'. Others expressed suspicion of 'informality in the classroom', of the role of the teacher as 'administrator/child minder', and reported a 'decrease in confidence as a teacher' and the accompanying strain. Some emphasized their 'traditionalist nature' and the disappointment suffered because they 'no longer had the great pleasure of teaching the top stream'.

Teachers commenting on the use of resource-based methods also emphasized the conflict these brought with their views of the teaching role: 'I spend a lot of time doing clerical work, preparation, marking, etc. I can't delude myself that this is teaching' (mathematics teacher).

iv. *Control*

Eight per cent of teachers referred to difficulties relating to control and discipline. These appeared to be associated with problems of providing suitable activities for all pupils and of meeting demands for attention as they arose. One teacher considered that a natural consequence of mixed ability grouping was that there were diruptive elements in every class. Control difficulties were fairly frequently referred to by heads of department; such comments were, however, most usually applied to probationer teachers who it might be argued may have encountered control problems whatever the organizational pattern. Indeed, a head of science with more than 10 years teaching experience described the difficulties as: 'The usual probationer problems with discipline', and it will be recalled that a very substantial proportion of teachers recorded *improved* behaviour as an outcome of mixed ability grouping.

(b) Institutional factors

Difficulties arising from what we have termed institutional factors – factors beyond the control of individual teachers – if not widespread, were identifiable in all areas. Foremost among such difficulties was class size, with a fifth of the teachers considering that the large size of their classes contributed to their difficulties. Seventeen per cent of teachers recorded problems resulting from the design and deployment of the buildings in which they worked, and the length of lesson units, timetable constraints and lack of money and equipment were each mentioned as difficulties by five per cent of the teachers of mixed ability classes.

i. *Class size*

Those teachers reporting difficulties arising from class size described their present classes as ranging from 20 (a woodwork class) to 40 pupils (a physical education group); the average size of class taught by these teachers was 32. A number talked in terms of an optimum class size and this on average was 20 pupils, although some spoke of as few as 15 and others thought 25 feasible. Points that were raised included the need to have a group size small enough to 'establish a personal relationship' and to avoid the problems associated with overcrowding in 'potentially hazardous' workshop and laboratory situations.

Few teachers attributed large class size to factors at work within their own institutions and an acceptance of the inevitability of large numbers was usual although one teacher from a school in which the administrative functions had been widely devolved suggested that the structure of the school organization was the cause of the problem – describing it as 'top heavy in terms of non-teaching staff'.

ii.   Buildings

Seventy teachers recorded difficulties arising from the design of the school buildings and how they were used. The way in which the 'school plant' was deployed was seen as a less critical factor than faults of design, although 11 teachers commented that difficulties arose from the failure to concentrate a department within an area or from the multiple use of rooms. Comments on the inadequacy of the teaching spaces focussed on such features as the small size of rooms, the lack of space for storage or display, the inflexibility of fixed bench layouts and the isolation from suitable storage areas even where these did exist.

iii.   Lesson length

The 20 teachers who described the length of the lesson as a constraint were evenly divided between those considering the unit to be too short (who reported an average lesson time of 38 minutes) and those considering the unit too long (average time reported, 77 minutes). Apart from one mathematician those teachers describing the lesson unit as too short came from the areas of aesthetic studies and humanities whereas those concerned with over-long lesson periods were from a range of disciplines – modern languages, home economics, science, art and the humanities. As reported in Chapter Three, experimentation with different lesson lengths was among the organizational changes associated with the introduction of mixed ability grouping in a number of schools.

iv.   Timetabling

Constraints imposed by the timetabling system were listed by five per cent of the teachers. Mixed ability teaching, concentrated as it is in the lower school, appeared particularly susceptible to 'fragmentation' and 'scattered isolated periods'; as one teacher put it – 'the timetable consumes mixed ability teaching'. The adoption of team teaching was rendered impossible in at least three of the schools, and the 'craft circus', with children moving from craft to craft at half termly intervals, also came under attack in others.

v. Money and equipment

Five per cent of those interviewed also commented that a lack of money contributed to their difficulties, bringing about shortage of texts, audio visual material, consumables and apparatus. Some teachers mentioning this difficulty occurred in half the schools in the sample.

5. Discussion

It was apparent that many of the teachers with whom we talked were making comparisons on the basis of their previous experience with streamed or setted groups or from their current experiences of such classes among older pupils. Whilst all but a few identified both advantages and disadvantages in having classes of mixed ability, certain groups of teachers displayed more favourable attitudes towards them than others. Factors associated with such attitudes, were explored at the beginning of this chapter and included training, length and nature of teaching experience, degree of involvement with mixed ability classes and teaching strategy. Those teachers whose initial training had contained elements concerned with mixed ability teaching were more likely to cite advantages than others. Attendance at in-service courses, on the other hand, did not appear to be related to how teachers viewed mixed ability work. Teachers who had the opportunity of meeting children from a wide range of ability through previous experience in a comprehensive school were more likely to cite advantages than those who had taught in selective schools, and our findings suggest that schools with relatively large numbers of probationers or teachers with ten or more years experience may face particular difficulties in seeking to introduce mixed ability grouping. These long service teachers are less likely to have received any preparation for mixed ability work in their initial training and may find it difficult to adapt to its demands. As important, they may find it difficult to support their younger colleagues. Whilst few (seven per cent) heads of departments which received mixed ability classes themselves taught only ability-selected groups, they were generally less involved with mixed ability groups than other staff (Chapter Two). Our evidence indicates that the more contact a teacher has with mixed ability classes the more likely he or she is to see advantages in them, although cause and effect cannot be disentangled here; it may simply be that those predisposed to them seek or are given more mixed ability classes to teach. Whilst over a third of the teachers who spent a considerable amount of time with mixed ability classes appeared to enjoy the challenge, reporting an increased satisfaction with their work, their comments have to be viewed alongside those voicing concern over the increased preparation and marking time, difficulties in securing and developing necessary resources and in meeting effectively each pupil's learning needs. It is apparent that mixed ability teaching had in some cases been introduced without adequate consideration of the skills and attitudes of the individual teachers whose task it was to implement it. Many teachers were in doubt concerning the teaching methodology to be adopted in classes where the spread of ability was wide and it was clear faced considerable difficulties in devel–oping or accepting a different role for themselves both in the class-room and in relation to their colleagues. The often noted ten-dency of teachers to isolate themselves and guard the privacy of their classroom life was evident in some instances and precluded the sharing of both experiences and resources.

The most commonly-cited advantage of having mixed ability groups was that these avoided the danger of labelling associated with selective grouping. As in other studies, advantages which may broadly be described as 'social' emerged as the major positive outcomes of mixed ability classes and teachers here drew attention to pupils' personal development, the improved classroom atmos-phere and increased co-operation among pupils and between pupils and teachers, with an accompanying decrease in disruptive be-haviour. Two points merit attention here, however; the first con-cerns our experience that many teachers were unable to specify the nature of the social benefits which they believed to be the outcome of unselective classes and were indeed frequently unwilling to explore this issue further. It may have been – and some teachers indeed said so – that the social benefits were so obvious that teachers considered further thought and investigation into their nature superfluous. There is, however, a danger that such advan-tages may be assumed. The second point concerns an irony; many teachers feel that the learning needs of their pupils cannot be met in mixed ability groups in the middle and later middle school years yet it is at this time when schools frequently most need strategies to improve the social fibre and contain disruption. It seems therefore that rarely can the greatest perceived advantage of mixed ability grouping be reaped at the time when it may be most needed.

The most widely-endorsed disadvantage of mixed ability teaching was that it led to a reduction in the motivation and achievement of the more able. Nearly 60 per cent of those teachers substantially involved with mixed ability classes made comments to this effect, thus echoing fears expressed elsewhere in the education service and the media. Again, however, it was difficult to get any real clarification as to the ways in which the achievement of the able was affected. It seems that a closer questioning as to the nature of the 'stretching' offered in a streamed class and apparently no longer available in an unselected group might serve to indicate how the needs of the abler students might more effectively be met.

A substantial proportion of teachers also recorded disadvantages for pupils at the lower end of the ability range but they were outnumbered by those who considered the less able to benefit from being in a mixed ability class, where they had the example in terms of both achievement and motivation of their more academically gifted peers and where they did not feel labelled and rejected. The problems, however, of coping with pupils lacking in basic skills and of ensuring that the learning tasks selected for these pupils offered them some opportunity for development, are well-evidenced in the comments reported in this chapter. In contrast, we have a dearth of evidence, a paucity of comment, specifically focussed on those children who form the majority of pupils in schools – the so-called 'average' pupils in the middle range of ability. Our data would sustain the interpretation that since very little mention was made of any disadvantages for this group and mixed ability teaching was perceived by many teachers as 'teaching to the middle' – that these pupils fare at least as well in mixed ability groups as in any kind of selected class. However, the sheer volume of comment focussed on other pupils – pupils at the extremes of the ability range – must alert us to the danger of the possibility of 'average' children being overlooked and the range of their individual differences being ignored.

Chapter Six

Subject Differences and Teaching Approaches

So far we have discussed teachers' views on the advantages and disadvantages of mixed ability teaching in general terms without reference to particular school subjects. Nor have we yet looked at the strategies teachers in different disciplines employ to meet the needs of pupils of widely varying abilities in one class. We reported in the last chapter that many teachers were unsure as to their role and the teaching approaches which they should adopt and, indeed, as the ILEA inspectorate (1976) stated: 'There appears to be general agreement that mixed ability teaching makes demands on techniques, methods, materials and standards markedly different from those operating in the schools in which teachers themselves were educated; different from those usually acquired in Colleges of Education and University Departments, at least until very recently; and different from those practised in schools where streaming or banding is the order of the day.'

What techniques and methods – different or otherwise – were teachers adopting with mixed ability classes? In the following pages we explore classroom practices in specific subject disciplines but begin by reviewing how far teachers considered their subjects to be suitable for teaching to mixed ability groups.

1. Perceptions of subject suitability – an overview
The subject categories outlined in Chapter Two and listed in Table 2.1A are used throughout this section to identify 'subject' teachers, and a distinction is drawn between 'main subject' teachers – a population of 469 – and a very small group of ten teachers with no readily identifiable main subject. These staff divided their teaching

96

between two or more departments in such a way that no one subject area received a majority of their time; indeed one teacher taught seven different subjects in the course of each week. The perceptions of teachers with no main subject are considered separately.

Teachers were asked during their interview whether they saw their subject as one which lent itself to a mixed ability approach. From the outset it was clear that replies to this question would require considerable probing and interpretation since certain assumptions about the nature of a subject and the nature of a mixed ability class influenced the way in which responses were made. The grouping of responses into subject categories enabled such assumptions to be examined, and provided some insight into teachers' perceptions of their subject and their aims and objectives in teaching mixed ability classes.

The question was put to all except teachers of special or remedial classes and no teacher felt unable to reply. Comments grounded in experience with mixed ability classes taught in a previous school year or in another school were accepted; in fact 52 teachers were not currently teaching any unstreamed groups, but when previous teaching experience was taken into account the numbers of staff who lacked experience of such groups dropped to 18. As all teachers who work in a school where mixed ability classes are a common form of organization will know, it is not possible to remain uninvolved for many weeks. With the first wave of winter 'flu a rapid acquaintance is made with all manner of hitherto unknown groups of children as substitution slips are handed out. Thus even if a department does not itself contain groups of mixed ability pupils, a teacher is likely to encounter such groups outside his regular timetabled programme and to be aware of ways in which they may or may not appear to differ from the sets, streams or bands with which he normally works. It was, therefore, considered valuable to include the perceptions of those teachers not substantially involved with mixed ability classes.

Initial responses to the question 'Do you consider that your subject lends itself to a mixed ability approach?' were classified in three categories; the 41 per cent of the sample who said 'Yes', the 21 per cent who replied 'No' and the remaining 38 per cent who considered that their subjects were suited in some respects to a mixed ability form of organization. Distinct subject differences were indicated and details of these appear in Table 6.1. All teachers

Table 6.1:   *Subject suitability for mixed ability teaching as perceived by subject teachers*

Subject Suitability	Main Subject (N = 456*)														Total N
	Aesthetic Subjects %	Commerce %	Domestic Studies %	English %	Integrated Humanities (with English) %	Integrated Humanities (without English) %	Non-integrated Humanities %	Language Studies %	Mathematics %	Music %	Physical Education %	Integrated Science %	Non-integrated Science %	Technical Studies %	
Suitable	79	14	21	61	100	92	57	11	14	27	70	38	36	35	189
Not suitable	8	0	8	3	0	0	8	56	47	27	11	23	14	19	95
Suitable in some Respects	13	86	71	36	0	8	35	33	39	46	19	39	50	46	172
Subject Teachers (N)	24	7	24	67	5	12	63	55	66	11	27	13	56	26	456

*NOTE: (a) Ten teachers with no main subject and 13 remedial teachers are excluded from this table

  (b) Percentages have been used in this table despite very small numbers in some instances; it is, therefore, essential to note the total number of teachers in each subject.

of integrated humanities with or without an English component, for example, perceived this subject as suitable at least in some respects for a mixed ability approach; in sharp contrast over half of the language teachers were emphatic that mixed ability classes were not suitable for modern language teaching. Scientists were less polarized in their views – approximately one-fifth of science teachers recorded a negative response and over one-third a positive one. The ideas which prompted such responses are examined in Section 3.

A very highly significant association was found between teachers' perceptions of subject suitability and the length of their teaching experience and, as might be expected from the results reported in Chapter Five, the large group of teachers with over ten years experience differed in their response from all other groups with fewer than a third considering their subject suitable for mixed ability teaching. We have also already commented on the highly significant association between the extent to which teachers were involved with mixed ability classes and their perceptions of subject suitability (Table 6.2).

Table 6.2: *Teachers' assessment of subject suitability and their involvement in teaching mixed ability classes*

Teacher perception of subject	Mixed ability as a percentage of teaching time				
	<50	51–85	86–99	100	
	%	%	%	%	%
Suitable	36	44	54	63	44
Suitable in some respects	43	39	36	28	39
Unsuitable	21	17	10	9	17
Total number of teachers (N)	194	92	31	78	395*

Non response 8
$x^2 = 18.60 \, p = <.01$

*(NOTE: This table excludes the 76 teachers who were not substantially involved in teaching ability-selected classes)

Less than a third of the very small group of teachers (16) whose only previous experience had been in grammar schools considered their subjects as suitable for mixed ability teaching; by contrast, the most favourable perceptions came from those 35 teachers whose previous teaching had been entirely in secondary modern schools, over half of whom regarded their subject as suitable. Of the 143 teachers whose only experience was in comprehensive or bilateral schools 48 per cent considered their subjects to lend themselves to a mixed ability approach.

2. Classroom organization

All teachers who were substantially involved with mixed ability groups were asked to detail the methods which they commonly employed in the course of teaching their main subject to a mixed ability class. A prompt card was used which listed the following methods:

Individual learning
Small groups (five and under)
Large groups (more than five)
Whole class as the teaching unit
Teaching unit of more than one class

Teachers were asked to indicate the frequency with which they used each on a five-point scale ranging from 'very frequently' to 'never'; Table 6.3 summarizes the information obtained from these interviews.

Table 6.3: *Teaching methods of main subject teachers in mixed ability classes*

	\multicolumn{6}{c}{Frequency of Use (N = 393)}				
Teaching Methods	Very Fre-quent	Fre-quent	Sometimes	Very Occasional	Never	All Teachers
Individual learning	80	93	56	54	110	393
Small groups	61	106	77	46	103	393
Large groups	11	55	62	64	201	393
Whole class	212	122	34	9	16	393
More than one class	13	19	43	70	248	393

(NOTE: Those ten teachers with no main subject are omitted from this table)

Each one of the five specified teaching methods was used in mixed ability classes and every subject was seen to provide some opportunity for a variety of teaching techniques. As noted in Chapter Five, the method of classroom organization used most frequently by those in the sample was whole class teaching. Fifty-four per cent of teachers used this method very frequently and a further 31 per cent adopted the method frequently, resulting in a total of 85 per cent of the sample for whom whole class teaching played an important part in classroom activities. Those members of staff who taught the whole class sometimes or very occasionally constituted 11 per cent of the sample and represented 11 of the 14 subjects. The 16 teachers who never taught the whole class represented only four per cent of the sample and were drawn from eight subject areas, with half of the responses coming from mathematics and home economics teachers.

With reference to Table 6.3 it should be noted that a teacher who records frequent or very frequent use of whole class teaching does not necessarily use this method as the dominant teaching mode. A teacher may use several teaching methods during the course of one lesson, and the balance may be such that none is dominant. In the context of this investigation a teacher is said to have a dominant teaching method when one mode is used frequently or very frequently and all others are used very occasionally or not at all. Fifty-four teachers (14 per cent of the sample) used whole class teaching as their dominant teaching mode according to this definition, and these are classified according to subject in Table 6.4. It will be noted that approximately one-third of modern language teachers used whole class teaching as their dominant mode of instruction.

The organization of small groups of pupils within the classroom was the second most common strategy, being used frequently or very frequently by 43 per cent of the sample, sometimes or very occasionally by 31 per cent and never by 26 per cent. Individual learning approaches were used with similar frequency, and these covered a wide variety of learning situations – using a language laboratory in modern language lessons, writing a poem or story in English, practising a skill in physical education, using a workcard in mathematics, sewing an apron in needlework – all activities which a pupil can pursue at his or her own pace with periodic guidance from the teacher. Only four teachers, however, used the individual learning approach as their dominant teaching mode (three mathematicians and one domestic studies teacher).

Groups containing more than five pupils ('large' groups) were used frequently or very frequently by only 17 per cent of subject teachers interviewed, sometimes or very occasionally by 32 per cent and not at all by 51 per cent of the sample; almost three-quarters of the English, integrated humanities and physical education teachers interviewed made use of large groups as compared with only one-third of home economics, mathematics and integrated science teachers. The nature of the subject clearly influences the use of large groups; the first three subjects offer scope for discussion, drama and team work of a kind which is not readily comparable with the practical and experimental activities encountered in home economics and science and with the individual nature of many tasks undertaken in mathematics. Group work, whether with large or small groups, was again very rarely (four instances) found as a teacher's dominant mode of teaching.

The fifth category, 'Teaching unit of more than one class', took many different forms. This question was not concerned with option classes where one teacher might indeed be teaching pupils from several different forms, but with situations where two or more pupil groups were working together with the involvement of two or more members of staff – an arrangement often referred to as 'team teaching'. There were 145 teachers from 13 subject areas who at some time taught more than one class; this mode of organization was therefore the least common of the five reviewed and only eight per cent of teachers made frequent or very frequent use of it. The 13 teachers claiming very frequent use were concerned with English, humanities, physical education and non-integrated science. Twenty-nine per cent of staff representing all subjects except commerce, taught more than one class sometimes or very occasionally.

Timetabled provision for team teaching included the following variations:
1. A humanities department with lessons 'blocked' to permit lead lessons and team preparation, but with one teacher permanently attached to each class.
2. A humanities department where staff co-operated in the preparation of lead lessons and resource materials for a series of topics within which pupils selected one activity for follow-up work, joining the appropriate group. This flexible system afforded pupils the opportunity of working with a number of different teachers.
3. A science department where three classes were timetabled

Table 6.4: *Teachers using whole class teaching as the dominant mode of classroom organization with mixed ability classes*

Subject	Dominant Class Teaching (N = 393)			
	Number of subject teachers	Incidence of dominant class teaching	Incidence as % of teachers per subject	Incidence as % of all subject teachers
Aesthetic subjects	24	3	12.5	0.8
Commerce	6	—	—	—
Domestic Studies	24	6	25.0	1.5
English	60	8	13.3	2.0
Integrated Humanities (with English)	5	—	—	—
Integrated Humanities (without English)	11	1	9.0	0.3
Non-integrated Humanities	57	7	12.3	1.8
Modern Languages	40	12	30.0	3.0
Mathematics	43	6	14.0	1.5
Music	11	2	18.2	0.5
Physical Education	27	—	—	—
Integrated Science	12	1	8.3	0.3
Non-integrated Science	49	3	6.1	0.8
Technical Studies	24	5	20.8	1.3
Total number of teachers (N)	393	54	—	13.8

together with an allocation of four teachers. The 'floating' teacher assisted pupils who were experiencing difficulties.

4. A faculty system whereby half a year group was block timetabled so that faculties were free to teach in mixed ability groups, to band, set, experiment in team teaching and in any other way desired. The resulting flexibility within faculties meant that there was a 'diverse team of staff available at one time' – to quote from the school's curriculum guide. This system also made possible 'large group lead sessions, team preparation, team teaching ... and integrated courses', while facilitating the organization of faculty staff meetings without disrupting the teaching programme.

5. A faculty system within which subject teachers worked together on the production of resource packages and in the presentation of lead lessons. After each lead lesson pupils returned to classrooms for follow-up work based on these resource kits. Weekly team meetings were timetabled and at the end of each topic one meeting was devoted to an evaluation of the unit's effectiveness.

3. Teachers' perceptions of subject suitability and their methods of classroom organization for mixed ability teaching

Our discussions with teachers highlighted marked differences in attitudes and teaching approaches among those in different subject disciplines. In the paragraphs which follow, three aspects of each subject are examined (i) its suitability for a mixed ability approach as perceived by teachers, (ii) methods of classroom organization and (iii) teaching strategies which staff identified as being particularly helpful in a mixed ability class.

Subjects are considered in turn following the rank order of positive responses to subject suitability in Table 6.1. As a common approach is adopted in the case of each, a certain degree of repetitiveness is inevitable; readers mainly interested in a particular subject area may find it useful to consult the contents section at the beginning of the report.

i. Integrated humanities

Teachers of integrated humanities recorded the highest percentage of positive responses to the subject suitability question and this subject area is therefore explored first. Twelve of the 17 staff concerned were teaching integrated humanities without English and the remaining five were teaching English as part of an integrated humanities course. There was no difference apparent in the nature of their response to this question. Only one member of staff teaching integrated humanities as a main subject expressed reservations as to its suitability for mixed ability groups.

Particular stress was laid on the social aspects of education, and the flexibility offered by a humanities programme within which discussion formed an important part and pupils were encouraged to contribute in their own way. 'All can work to the limit of their potential' and 'All can contribute' were two comments supportive of this view. Several teachers stressed the importance of enjoyment as a motivational force and felt that this could be achieved by a judicious selection of topics. In discussion work the comment 'It is important to have a variety of opinions in moral studies discussions' was reinforced by another teacher who welcomed discussion work 'because it is useful to have wide personal as well as educational standards'. Perceived social benefits were generally related to the methods of classroom organization employed by the teacher, summed up by the member of staff who stated 'Content is not really important, it is how it's taught that matters'. Throughout it was apparent that teachers of humanities were concerned with all aspects of the child's development and they saw this subject area as providing learning opportunities suited to the individual requirements of each child; the subject was considered to encompass a 'wide variety of material' and to contain concepts that 'can be dealt with at very different levels' and within which 'individualized learning is the keynote'. The sole reservation centred on one teacher's concern over children who lacked basis language skills and had difficulties with certain of the written aspects of the humanities course.

Table 6.5: *Teaching methods: integrated humanities*

Teaching Method	Very Frequent	Frequent	Sometimes	Very Occasional	Never	All Teachers
Individual learning	4	5	4	1	2	16
Small groups	1	5	3	4	3	16
Large groups	1	2	2	7	4	16
Whole class	10	4	1	1	0	16
More than one class	0	2	7	4	3	16

Frequency of Use (N = 16)

Table 6.5 indicates that the two most frequently used organizational modes were whole class teaching and individual learning; class teaching was used frequently or very frequently by 14 staff and individual learning frequently or very frequently by nine. Small groups, large groups and groups of more than one class were organized for integrated humanities lessons, but fewer teachers made very frequent use of these methods in comparison with individual and whole class approaches.

Whole class teaching was the only technique employed by every staff member interviewed and this method was mentioned specifically in conjunction with lesson introductions, giving instructions and discussing points which pupils were finding difficult. In a team teaching system, class teaching sometimes constituted the follow-up to a lead lesson once pupils returned to their own classroom. Individual learning was perceived as appropriate for topic and project work, for follow-up exercises after fieldwork and for studies guided by worksheets. The nature of individual work evidently varied a great deal as it was observed that teachers were happy to allow pupils to progress at their own speed on a project but expected members of the class to reach much the same point at a given time when following a communal work sheet. Constraints of preparation time and resource materials were mentioned as restricting more extensive use of individual learning techniques.

Groups were used by 14 of the 16 teachers interviewed, small groups being used more frequently than large groups of five or more pupils. Teachers influenced group structures in 10 out of the 14 cases cited, taking pupils' ability, the nature of the topic and existing friendship patterns into consideration. Opinion varied as to the role of the latter; one teacher considered it the most important factor particularly in a subject 'where pupils are discussing, arguing and debating in groups'; another reported that he sometimes led pupils out of friendship groups 'so that individuals can be coaxed into making their own choices', thus recognizing the possible constraints that peer allegiances may exert on academic and personal development.

Teaching groups consisting of more than one class were encountered by 13 of the 16 humanities staff, but never very frequently. Examples were quoted of classes joining together on fieldwork expeditions, to watch a film or to participate in a lead lesson introducing a new topic or theme.

ii.   Aesthetic studies

Approximately four-fifths of the staff who taught art considered their subject suitable for a mixed ability approach. Further exploration revealed a concept fundamental to the teaching of aesthetic subjects which had strongly influenced responses; the majority of art teachers did not consider that ability – perceived to be of an academic nature – was generally reflected in a pupil's artistic aptitude. Frequent reference was made to the fact that the development of an individual aptitude was a central objective of art teaching – 'we are seeking to develop powers of expression through materials'. In art there were 'no set answers' and even examinations assessed where the pupil was in his work rather than 'how much he had in his head'. Several teachers emphasized the importance of social interaction and the advantages of flexible forms of classroom organization. Pupils were usually free to sit and to move where they wished, learning from each other as well as being guided by the teacher.

The views of teachers who did not support mixed ability art provided insight into a different set of aims and objectives. These teachers clearly perceived something approaching an absolute standard in art and were keen that pupils should develop individually towards this goal. In appropriately graphic terms the team were told that in a mixed ability class a 'greyness develops' and that 'the sparklers don't shine' despite a great deal of personal attentions. The 'greyness' did not appear to represent a general lowering of standards of the more able; it was perceived as a 'sameness', a lack of depth and originality in individual pieces of work at any level. The view was expressed that in art pupils 'do better' when grouped with others of similar ability but no definition was offered as to how this achievement was to be measured or in what direction progress was to be made.

In art, craft and design whole class teaching and individual learning were the two methods used by the greatest number of staff and also the only two methods which were used very frequently (Table 6.6). The links between these two methods were clear, for, as one teacher pointed out, 'There is a common theme and a common jumping off point. Individual work is convenient as pupils can work in different media.'

Teachers considered the structure of each lesson to be important for if a topic were flexible and instructions simple, all could embark on the task, leaving the teacher free to assist with specific problems: 'I set relatively simple tasks and the work is carefully structured.' Thus it was common for teachers to address the whole class together at the start of a lesson and then to arrange for pupils to proceed with individual or sometimes group assignments. Class teaching towards the end of the lesson was designed to ensure that all necessary clearing up was carried out. Three art teachers used class teaching so extensively that it dominated all classroom activities.

Eighteen of the 24 staff used groups at some stage and over half of these were formed by pupils and teacher together. Teachers considered friendship the most important factor to be taken into account, closely followed by ability (one teacher stressed again that this was artistic ability and not academic ability), the nature of the topic and class control. Group work was mentioned in conjunction with designing and painting murals, making table games and constructing papier maché masks and models.

Table 6.6:   *Teaching methods: aesthetic subjects*

Teaching Method	Very Fre-quent	Fre-quent	Sometimes	Very Occasional	Never	All Teachers
Individual learning	9	8	0	2	5	24
Small groups	0	3	3	8	10	24
Large groups	0	4	1	5	14	24
Whole class	13	8	2	0	1	24
More than one class	0	1	2	4	17	24

Frequency of Use (N = 24)

Only seven teachers met groups of more than one class, an organizational mode which was considered appropriate in this subject for lead lessons and for viewing films.

iii.   Physical education

Almost three–quarters of those who taught physical education considered this subject entirely suited to a mixed ability approach; one-fifth saw both problems and possibilities while only one-tenth regarded the subject as totally unsuitable for mixed ability classes. The majority of teachers did not accept that ability in 'academic' subjects was necessarily associated with a pupil's physical ability, and any class, whether streamed, banded, setted or of mixed ability, was seen as comprising pupils with widely differing physical abilities. In this sense, physical education had always contained a mix of ability, and unstreaming was perceived as generally having little effect.

Whilst most physical education teachers had as the main aim of their teaching the development of a pupil's individual aptitude in their subject area, there was some evidence of awareness of conflicting demands; this was apparent in the comment of one teacher who asked 'Am I teaching social co-operation or standards?' It would appear that where the former is the aim, problems are relatively few, since work in pairs, groups and teams are part of traditional teaching strategy in physical education. Difficulties were perceived as arising when an attempt was made to develop pupils' vastly differing individual skills to one specified level of physical competence. Swimming was cited as one example and gymnastics another. In both these activities teachers felt that work on a one to one basis was the only feasible way to developing a pupil's skills. A class of mixed academic ability was not regarded as easing or exacerbating this particular difficulty; it was a problem perceived as inherent in the nature of the subject. Where the range of academic ability in a class did influence the course of a lesson, however, was during team games. Several teachers considered the more academically able to be 'better players in the sense that their tactical skills are often superior to those of the less academically able pupils'. In games the pupil with good tactics frequently scored over the pupil whose physical co-ordination was in fact better but whose planning capacity was less well developed.

Table 6.7:   *Teaching methods: physical education*

Teaching Method	Very Fre-quent	Fre-quent	Sometimes	Very Occasional	Never	All Teachers
	Frequency of Use (N = 27)					
Individual learning	3	10	4	3	7	27
Small groups	8	15	2	1	1	27
Large groups	4	16	2	3	2	27
Whole class	9	14	2	1	1	27
More than one class	8	3	4	4	8	27

Teaching organization in physical education resembled the overall pattern in the proportion of teachers making frequent or very frequent use of whole class teaching but differed from it in the much more extensive use of large and small groups (Table 6.7).

Class teaching was used to outline the structure of a lesson, to demonstrate a particular skill or technique and to instruct pupils in the procedures to be followed. Of those who used groups in their teaching, two-thirds created them in conjunction with the pupils and the most frequently considered factors were pupils' abilities and the nature of the topic on which they were to work. Friendships were sometimes taken into account, but other factors emerged – e.g. the physical size of individual pupils influenced teachers' decisions as to who was placed where on the netball court or rugby field and in apparatus work in the gym. Five of the seven teachers who left pupils to select their own groups observed that they sorted themselves out by physical ability. Small groups or pairs were commonly used for practising skills and large groups for games, dance and activities based on team competition.

Teachers were aware that because pupils' abilities differed, in some instances separate activities might be appropriate, and, of the 18 teachers who expressed this view, in fact two 'streamed' within the classroom. One teacher saw the role of lunchtime clubs and school teams as complementary to classwork; this teacher spent more time with the less able pupil during lessons but gave the more able attention in lunch hour club activities and in team practices, claiming that 'the teacher pupil relationship is built up then'.

Groups of more than one class were strongly represented in the responses, reflecting the common practice of timetabling two or more forms together for physical education lessons and then dividing pupils into teaching groups of the same sex. This system was seen to make the best use of staff and of teaching space.

iv.   *English*

The precise nature of English as a subject proved difficult to define. Although 'English' formed part of the core curriculum of all the schools in the sample, it presented as many facets as there were teachers. Almost two-thirds of the teachers considered that English lent itself to a mixed ability approach, approximately one-third felt that it presented problems as well as possibilities and two English teachers stated that the subject was not suited in any way for teaching to classes with a wide range of ability.

The subject was perceived by many teachers to be 'fluid', 'flexible' and in the first three years essentially free from the restrictions of a prescriptive syllabus. Mixed ability groups were considered to be both feasible and desirable during the early years of secondary school when a wide choice of themes and topics was available within which each child could contribute at a level appropriate to his ability. This emphasis on the pupil's individual development was made by the majority of English teachers interviewed and the subject was seen as providing opportunity for the use of a variety of stimulus material to which the pupil could respond in an individual way. Discussion and debate, drama and other forms of creative activity were all employed to motivate and to maintain the interest of pupils. It was considered possible for very different abilities to produce work from the same stimulus material, while the availability of a 'vast number of topics' was regarded as helpful to the teacher in maintaining interest and enjoyment for pupils of different abilities.

Within this wide range of themes, topics and projects teachers used different forms of classroom organization to encourage co-operation and an exchange of ideas among pupils. Drama, story-telling, creative writing, discussion, debate and poetry reading were all seen as offering opportunities for pupils to work together in 'a sharing process' within a subject in which 'communication is everything'. In discussion periods a mixed ability class was considered particularly helpful since it provided 'a wide range of experience and different backgrounds' which lent a richness to discussion not experienced by teachers in a streamed or setted situation. As one teacher explained 'Segregation impoverishes children of experience of each other'. Discussion emerged as a central feature of English lessons and was perceived as a means whereby all pupils could take part, developing skills of logical argument and acquiring an awareness and understanding of the viewpoint of others. Emphasis on the socializing role of English was strong. 'The class is its own resource – a social microcosm' explained one teacher who saw mixed ability English classes as providing the ideal situation in which to develop pupils' social skills and attitudes. 'English is social and linguistic and with mixed ability classes a representative mix is achieved'. Similar perceptions held by another teacher were that 'academic and socializing roles are inseparable in English'. 'Both language and literature enable children to test ideas and thoughts'. English literature was considered to provide opportunities for pupils to seek parallels with present day human situations and to lend depth to work at all levels. Mixed ability English was considered to facilitate co-operative endeavour and teachers frequently encouraged pupils who had mastered a particular skill to aid those who were still struggling.

Reservations centred on two areas – the child who was lacking in basic skills, and the pressures of examinations in the fifth year. Teachers considered that individual and independent progress in English depended on the pupil first attaining certain basic literacy skills; weakness in these presented a child with endless difficulties. The mixed ability classroom was not regarded as providing the most suitable environment in which to assist pupils who lacked basic reading and writing skills. Concerning the second area, examinations, little mention was made of syllabus or course content until the fourth and fifth years. The subject was perceived as 'not content-based' and 'not fact-dominated' and one teacher referring to first year English studies was adamant that teaching 'must not follow precise patterns'. However, when formal grammar was introduced into fourth and fifth year mixed ability work, teachers found that some pupils had difficulty in coping. It was considered by some staff that the demands of an external examination could not be met within a mixed ability class, and setting was deemed a more suitable method of organization. Literacy was also raised as a problem in these later years – pupils' difficulties with examination work were compounded if at fourth and fifth year level they were still struggling to master basic skills.

The few teachers who saw English as a sequential language skill did not consider that a mixed ability group provided the most suitable environment for teaching pupils whose aptitudes and abilities would necessarily be very different. These teachers appreciated the social gains of mixed ability English but were uncertain as to the academic benefits. In summary, there was widespread agreement that English in the first three years lent itself to a mixed ability approach, with evidence of increasing reservations among teachers thereafter.

Sixty of the 67 English teachers in the sample were involved with mixed ability classes at the time of our enquiry. All of these 60 teachers used whole class teaching and all but three made frequent or very frequent use of this method (Table 6.8), usually for story-telling, poetry reading, giving instructions, using a class reader,

Table 6.8: *Teaching methods: English*

Teaching Method	Very Frequent	Frequent	Sometimes	Very Occasional	Never	All Teachers
			Frequency of Use (N = 60)			
Individual learning	5	14	12	12	17	60
Small groups	9	17	19	8	7	60
Large groups	2	4	19	19	16	60
Whole class	28	29	2	1	0	60
More than one class	1	2	10	9	38	60

introducing a new topic and for dealing with specific points of difficulty. Indeed, for eight members of staff class teaching was the dominant organizational mode. Teachers considered it important to involve all pupils in a common activity from time to time. Some teachers who had experienced problems in class teaching had managed to reduce these by 'pitching lower' at the start of the lesson. In this way, the attention and interest of all pupils was captured initially, and, provided the period of class teaching was not lengthy, all could be involved. A number of teachers, however, found discussion difficult to conduct in a mixed ability class.

The essence of English was seen to be a sharing of experience; all pupils were encouraged to contribute to classroom activities. Vocabulary work of a general nature was seen to be promoted by oral discussion, while a shared experience such as watching a film or listening to a poem was perceived to be a useful way of stimulating discussion and of exploring pupils' attitudes and opinions. Pupils learned from each other and when the class was taught as a whole the teacher could both guide discussions and introduce new vocabulary where appropriate. Discussion was viewed as an important exercise for encouraging pupils to express their ideas clearly. Comprehension on the other hand, was to be avoided as 'the dull can't do it and the bright find it boring'.

Some schools in the sample contained a high intake of immigrants for whom English was not the mother tongue. Consequently teachers were faced with a linguistic barrier and in this sought common ground, selecting topics of a general nature, such as 'the media', which were seen to provide a suitable meeting point for all pupils.

Groups work followed class teaching as the second most widely-used method in English, with 55 of the 60 teachers making use of groups at some time. Three quarters of these teachers influenced the structure of such groups, taking into account friendship patterns (25), ability (21), the nature of the topic (15) and less frequently other factors such as leadership qualities, misbehaviour and laziness. On those occasions when pupils selected their own groups in English, teachers generally perceived no regular pattern in the resulting mix of ability. Small groups were commonly used for project work, poetry reading, discussions and drama. Large groups, used by fewer teachers, were mentioned in connection with project work and drama.

Concern over standards was apparent in the upper school, where teachers sometimes varied the nature of groups within the classroom to cater for specific needs. Six teachers, for example, mentioned that they used groups based on ability during the term preceding external examinations in order to give pupils remedial consolidation or extension work as considered appropriate. In one school, a group of those identified as 'more able' was extracted for four weeks to make an intensive study of a Shakespearian play; in another, pupils were grouped by ability and set work at different levels within the same classroom. Thus, while these groups cannot be called 'mixed ability' groups, they formed part of the normal teaching strategy employed within a mixed ability class.

Individual learning techniques were used by approximately two-thirds of English teachers and included the writing of stories, essays and poems, silent reading, research on a given topic and individual remedial tuition which usually meant that the pupils left the classroom for part or all of the lesson. It was considered helpful to liaise with the remedial department so that appropriate work could be given to less able pupils and their progress monitored in 'regular' English lessons.

Only five of the 60 teachers of mixed ability English interviewed mentioned worksheets. One teacher, determined to avoid 'death by worksheet', was concentrating on adapting existing material for use with groups. Another found particular benefit in using the Science

Research Associates (SRA) workcards for a limited period as pupils enjoyed the competitive element as well as the change of activity which these afforded. From the teacher's viewpoint the SRA scheme was also considered advantageous as it gave the teacher an opportunity of 'keeping tabs' on pupils and becoming well acquainted with their specific linguistic aptitudes and weaknesses. It seems, however, that workcards were regarded as a peripheral rather than central part of classroom activities.

The importance of pupils taking responsibility for their own work and being able to use available resources independently was stressed. Project work was considered appropriate for all pupils in years one and two and for the less able pupil at all levels. Individualizing work and giving the pupils a choice of activities was advocated; in the words of one teacher, 'Allow their own motivation to select the work they do – stories, plays, punctuation cards, games. Variety is essential.'

Only one-third of English teachers were involved in team teaching, and the range of specified activities was small. Several classes or a whole year group were drawn together from time to time for a lead lesson, television programme or film. One teacher expressed concern over the ease with which the activities and progress of an individual pupil could be lost sight of where team teaching was employed.

Resource materials for English were not generally perceived to be in short supply; the chief difficulty lay in organizing existing resources so that they were readily accessible to both staff and pupils when required. Most rooms contained a class library, and some departments had developed indexing systems for the storage and retrieval of materials. Others, more recently introduced to mixed ability teaching, were planning to pool existing resource materials in the coming terms.

v. Non-integrated humanities
As noted in Chapter Two the range of subjects in non-integrated humanities was wide but the greatest number of responses in the sample came from teachers of religious education, history and geography; perceptions as to the nature of each subject proved more contentious than elsewhere. Over half of the staff teaching non-integrated humanities to mixed ability classes considered that their subject lent itself to this form of organization, five teachers

were adamant that it did not, while the remaining third said that some aspects were suited and others were not.

Discussion was considered by religious education teachers to be an essential part of any course, and work was usually organized into topics within which pupils could work at their own level. One teacher considered that 'streaming is not consistent with religious belief'. But the expression of ideas concerning belief and the ability to discuss moral issues was seen to involve a grasp of concepts and of language which all children did not possess. Thus discussions which formed an integral part of religious education lessons were encountering conceptual difficulties by the third year, when teachers were attempting to cater for pupils whose conceptual powers were at very different stages of development. But the vast majority of religious education teachers perceived value in a mixed ability organization which provided pupils with a learning experience within which they could learn from each other and in which there was a wide range of acceptable responses.

History teachers reflected a similar pattern of perception. In the first two years teachers saw history variously as a 'story', as a 'set syllabus' and as a subject for resource-based teaching and well suited to mixed ability classes, but there was general acceptance that around the third or fourth year the divergence in pupils' attitudes, interests and abilities became too wide in such classes for a teacher to cater for. Resource materials were seen to play a very important part in history teaching at all levels. The development of techniques of inquiry rather than the learning of facts was emphasized strongly and teachers saw in history many opportunities for structuring learning in order to achieve this objective.

The teachers who saw problems in teaching history to mixed ability classes were concerned over basic reading skills and conceptual development linked with the pupils' understanding of vocabulary. 'History must involve reading' contrasted with the 'changing resources and methods – Jackdaws, films, slides' approach adopted by teachers who did consider the subject as suited to a mixed ability approach.

Beyond the third year the increasing complexity of the ideas involved was seen to make demands which not all pupils in a mixed ability class could meet. Complexity was deemed a necessity since examinations were perceived as exerting considerable influence after the third year and pupils required a vocabulary and level of understanding which could deal with abstract concepts. One history teacher concerned with the practicalities of teaching a mixed ability class considered a mixed ability approach unsuitable where a class contained on the one hand potential good O-level candidates and on the other 'a bunch of assorted truants, disruptives, anti-socials and maladjusteds'. The provision of a variety of materials was seen as no solution since 'it is as much as most children can do to cope with *one* text book, never mind several'.

In geography, teachers' views were similarly polarized. On the one hand some teachers perceived the subject to be 'purely cultural' dealing with a series of topics and concerned with 'ideas not skills' while others were convinced that geography was 'becoming more of a science involving essential concepts of scale, direction and distance and containing lots of specialized names'. The first group of teachers without exception saw geography as lending itself well to mixed ability classes where it was possible to design topics which met pupils' needs and the subject was so flexible that a wide variety of resources and modes of classroom organization ensured the involvement of everyone. Group work and discussion constituted an important part of the work, and resources of all kinds were considered necessary in order to widen pupils' experience. It was felt that every child could contribute at some level to each topic although it was recognized that certain pupils had an aptitude for particular kinds of activity so individual progress was likely to be variable, depending on the nature of the activity.

The teachers who saw geography as a scientific discipline, and wished to teach it as such, experienced difficulties even in the first year with pupils' differential rates of progress. Failure of less able pupils to master essential techniques of measurement and recording and their apparent inability to comprehend the concepts of scale, distance, height, temperature and humidity were cited as examples of difficulties encountered by teachers in first year mixed ability classes. In the upper school, external examinations influenced a number of teachers, who considered that setting would enable geographical work to proceed at a pace appropriate to the pupil's level of conceptual understanding and would maximize his chance of examination success.

Recurring throughout the area of non-integrated humanities teaching were comments which showed that the perceived nature of each subject influenced the degree to which teachers considered it

possible to realize their aims and objectives in a mixed ability class.
As a group of subjects, the humanities offered scope for resource-
based learning, providing a variety of topics and themes, but
differences in pupils' literacy skills and rates of conceptual development were perceived to create difficulties in mixed ability
humanities work beyond the first or second year.

Fifty-seven of the 63 teachers of non-integrated humanities
interviewed were currently concerned with mixed ability classes.
The teaching methods reported indicated that whole class teaching
and individual learning were the two most widely used methods in
these subjects, with 46 out of the 57 staff members making frequent
or very frequent use of class teaching and 29 of the 57 making
similar use of individual learning (Table 6.9).

Table 6.9:   *Teaching methods: non-integrated humanities*

Teaching Method	Very Frequent	Frequent	Sometimes	Very Occasional	Never	All Teachers
Individual learning	14	15	10	10	8	57
Small groups	6	11	15	15	7	57
Large groups	0	6	10	5	36	57
Whole class	31	15	8	1	2	57
More than one class	1	6	6	14	30	57

(Frequency of Use, N = 57)

Class teaching was used at the start of a lesson 'to set the scene' or
to issue instructions, and also for short periods during a lesson as
required to meet pupils' needs. Teaching the whole class was seen to
assist in 'getting through the basic work' involved in history and
geography classes and to be a suitable technique for discussion in
religious education. A history teacher maintained that class teaching was particularly important because the vocabulary involved in
this type of exchange benefited the pupils by widening their experience. Class teaching dominated the work of eight of the humanities
staff interviewed.

Techniques of individual learning included worksheets structured to contain 'basic information and questions with which most

pupils can cope but which the less able don't always finish', and worksheets in which 'all in the class are kept together and the more able are given extra work'. The question may be posed, however, as to whether either system can be construed as providing an individual programme of learning for each pupil. One teacher saw homework as providing the opportunity for individual aptitudes and abilities to be developed. Tasks were open-ended so that in a 30-minute homework, for example, pupils might draw part of the Bayeux tapestry or write a short essay on a related topic. She noted that 'some don't do their best if the task is too simple', hence the need to provide a variety of homework exercises.

Groups were used by 43 teachers, the majority of whom (33) structured these in consultation with pupils. Factors taken into consideration by staff included friendship, ability, the nature of the topic and class control. Half of the teachers interviewed observed that when pupils selected their own working groups they chose to work with others of similar ability. As one historian remarked, 'they stream themselves'. The use of groups was varied. Geographers organized groups for fieldwork and mapwork, an historian used groups for drama, while in religious education one teacher appointed 'natural leaders', each to be responsible for the work of a pupil group.

One humanities teacher asked all pupils to sit in the same place for the duration of each topic. Books appropriate to the levels of children at each table were given out at the start of the topic. Pupils collected the same books at the start of each subsequent lesson and work could progress smoothly, leaving the teacher free to move from group to group. This teacher stressed the importance of leaving pupils to work without interruption throughout a lesson if they so desired, and for this reason any formal teaching was completed at the start of the lesson.

About half of the teachers encountered pupil groups comprising more than one class at some stage of their teaching. These situations ranged from regular fortnightly gatherings to termly or half-termly events and included the team teaching of 'promotion' or lead lessons to launch a new topic and the showing of films. In some cases, teachers reported that team teaching was constrained by timetabling and the availability of a large classroom or hall.

vi. Science

Forty-three of the 56 teachers whose main subject was non-integrated sciences also taught integrated science, combined science or general science to a mixed ability class in the lower school, and seven of the 13 main-subject integrated scientists also taught a non-integrated science subject. Responses from teachers of all science subjects will be examined together in the paragraphs which follow, with reference to specific areas being made where appropriate.

Over one third of science teachers considered their subject suitable for a mixed ability approach and almost half saw it as suitable in some respects. Perceptions as to the nature of science included emphasis on practical experimentation and the ease with which units or topics could be identified in all branches of the discipline. Indeed, a topic approach was employed by science teachers throughout the sample. Difficulties were concerned chiefly with conceptual development, language skills and the influence exerted by external examinations. Other difficulties were seen as arising not from the nature of the subject but from local constraints imposed by the school, staffing or the timetable.

Some teachers in each of biology, physics, combined, general and integrated science considered that the high practical and experimental content of each subject rendered it particularly suitable for mixed ability teaching. This, combined with a topic approach, provided units of study in which the pupil had the opportunity to work at his own level and pace. Involvement and enthusiasm on the part of the pupil was a clearly-stated aim, and teachers experienced little difficulty in achieving this in mixed ability science in the early years of secondary education. By emphasizing the development of skills 'and by not leaning too heavily on the learning of facts, science can easily be taught to mixed ability classes – particularly with the aim of enthusing kids and providing a good basis for future work in science'. Science subjects were perceived as requiring the use of many different skills, and it was accepted that pupils would exhibit varying degrees of competence. One teacher voiced this as follows – 'Science has different levels, it is custom-made for mixed ability teaching. Experiments can be conducted at different levels, even on the same topic.' However, if the teacher is to accept different rates of progress and development from his pupils, he will have to know each child personally in order to assess when the time is right to start a different topic or to introduce a new concept into an existing unit of study.

Reservations were expressed by many teachers over the continuation of mixed ability science into the fourth and fifth years. Some teachers, indeed, could not accept the prospect of mixed ability science beyond the first year although the majority considered that mixed ability science in the first three years was feasible. Problems arose initially with the introduction of certain concepts in the second year. In mixed ability classes there were found to be children who did not understand the principles involved in a particular stage of the work. Literacy and numeracy were considered essential tools for scientific work, particularly from the second year onwards, and teachers considered that pupils without these skills were unable to contribute fully towards the work and unable to gain from it.

Physicists in particular encountered difficulties due to pupils' lack of mathematical understanding as early as the second year which, compounded with the slow development of abstract thought in the less able children, made the task of physics teaching very difficult. The appropriate balance between experimental and theoretical work was perceived to differ considerably for those who could grasp the theoretical concepts and those who could not, thus producing problems of classroom organization.

Restrictions imposed by the examination syllabus were deemed to exert a profound influence in the upper school. Mode 3 had been adopted in some cases as a means of overcoming these restrictions, but it alleviated rather than solved pupils' conceptual problems. Although some teachers deplored the social effects of streaming for CSE and GCE they considered that the academic and conceptual demands of science courses at this level could not be met adequately in mixed ability classes.

Table 6.10: *Teaching methods: science*

Teaching Method	Frequency of Use (N = 61)					
	Very Frequent	Frequent	Sometimes	Very Occasional	Never	All Teachers
Individual learning	4	13	10	7	27	61
Small groups	26	25	4	3	3	61
Large groups	0	3	9	12	37	61
Whole class	28	20	9	2	2	61
More than one class	1	1	4	16	39	61

Sixty-one of the 69 science teachers interviewed taught mixed ability classes, and Table 6.10 shows the methods they used to organize their classrooms. Greatest and most frequent use was made of class teaching and small groups; individual learning was used by 34 of the 61 teachers, large groups by 24 and team teaching involved 22 teachers, 16 of whom stated that this took place very occasionally. Class teaching dominated in four cases, group work in three, but the majority of teachers used a variety of teaching methods.

Fifty-nine teachers used groups at some stage in their teaching and over half constructed these in conjunction with the pupils. In only four cases did the teacher exercise complete control over group structure. Factors taken into consideration were friendship, classroom control and the ability of individual pupils. Other factors were mentioned less frequently – the availability of apparatus and the nature of the topic, for example. Twenty-three teachers allowed pupils to select their own working groups and about half of these teachers commented that these were groups of like ability. In the first year groups tended to be based on primary school friendships and the mix of ability was often wide. With time, however, groups changed and by the second or third year most were based on ability with, as one biologist noted, 'the brighter ones working together and competing with each other'.

It was clear that groups formed an important part of science teaching. Small groups were used almost exclusively for experimental work, and teachers preferred to have two or possibly three pupils working together. In this way each child could participate usefully in the work undertaken. Small groups were contrived to secure 'personal compatibility', as one teacher explained. In another classroom the teacher always made sure that there was 'someone who could read' in each group and further comments about group structure indicated that staff who tried to achieve a mix of ability in each group did this to encourage co-operation and to avoid certain pupils being 'left behind'. Large groups were generally regarded as an expedient to be used in certain circumstances – lack of apparatus was quoted as one instance where it was necessary to have pupil groups with more than five members for experimental work.

Class teaching was considered appropriate for short periods, generally at the start and finish of a lesson in order to organize pupils and at intervals during the lesson to comment on progress or to clear up a point on which pupils needed further assistance.

Periods of about ten minutes were quoted as the norm, but longer sessions of class teaching were sometimes used, for example, in the teaching of scientific skills and of 'rules' for working in a laboratory. The provision of a variety of resource materials was considered important for laboratory work and frequent mention was made of the invaluable assistance given by laboratory technicians in this respect. Worksheets and graded workcards were used and considerable emphasis was placed on the use of equipment kits and trays, and display materials. Only two staff members, however, considered worksheets to be suitable for the whole ability range, and one teacher refuted their use at any stage on the grounds that they were 'no good' for coping with pupils' conceptual difficulties in science. More than half of the staff used individual learning techniques at some stage and it was considered that individual participation could be achieved readily by means of experimental work, which a pupil might undertake as a group member or on his own. Guidance by the teacher in this situation reassured the pupil and permitted the teacher to 'keep tabs' on individual pupils' progress. Of the courses available, Nuffield science was regarded as the most appropriate for unstreamed classes.

A teaching pattern which recurred was class teaching for introductory sessions, followed by group work or individual tasks, perhaps guided by work sheets and most successful if worksheets were graded and open ended. Conceptual problems could be discussed as they arose, on an informal basis with the teacher, and pupils were perceived to gain since the teacher was more accessible.

Concern for the less able pupil was voiced by more than one-third of science teachers. It was considered helpful to provide a variety of activities within science lessons so that every pupil could find something to do which was of interest, relevant to the topic and which was within his capabilities. The less able were seen to be motivated more towards the practical aspects of science, but it was noted that these pupils required frequent changes of topic in order to maintain a positive attitude towards the subject. One teacher provided a set of equipment and a handwritten sheet for each of the less able pupils to use in class. The instruction sheets were simple and contained information for one task only – characteristics regarded as important for all worksheets used in a class where some pupils were known to have reading difficulties. Stress was laid on the importance of relating the work in hand to the pupils' own experience wherever possible and 'talking to them about the work in their own language'. This was seen to be particularly relevant in a mixed ability class where not all pupils were able to understand technical explanations. One science teacher, a head of department, found it helpful to look at each topic from the point of view of the 'weakest' pupils. He then structured the unit, making the 'first part of the work something they can all manage', and providing extension material for the more able. He found that reducing the written components helped, and made wide use of demonstrations and blackboard illustrations. Pupils were encouraged to make their own notes on experiments and to supplement these with diagrams and charts from the blackboard. Five of the 22 staff who expressed concern about the less able pupils reported that they had found no way of resolving the difficulties presented by such pupils in mixed ability classes.

The most usual way of meeting the needs of the more able was by means of graded and open-ended worksheets in the first instance, then by personal guidance from the teacher who directed pupils towards appropriate extension work. One-third of the teachers who reported concern over the more able pupils in science had still to find an adequate way of meeting their needs.

Teaching groups of more than one class were organized in a number of schools where the timetable 'blocked' science periods, so that lead lessons, team teaching, films and fieldwork could be organized on a departmental basis.

vii.   Technical studies

Teachers of technical subjects were divided over the perceived suitability of their subject for a mixed ability approach. Approximately one-third viewed their subject as suitable, almost half considered that it presented problems as well as possibilities, while the remaining fifth of the teachers interviewed felt craft to be unsuitable in every way for mixed ability teaching. Many teachers' perceptions were similar to those expressed by teachers of art. The distinctions made earlier about 'academic ability' differing from 'practical ability' were reiterated by technical teachers – 'we have always been mixed ability' – although a link was recognized between general ability and success in technical work at a more advanced stage where demands on literacy and numeracy were high.

Woodwork, metalwork and technical drawing were the chief subject areas represented and teachers saw each subject as providing opportunity for the development of individual practical skills. It was considered important for pupils to receive individual guidance, and teachers encouraged children to take responsibility for their own learning programme and approach the teacher for aid as required. Speed was regarded as 'immaterial' and stress placed on each pupil being able to proceed at his own pace. Staff considered that in technical subjects all pupils had something to offer – 'everyone can do something' – and as long as there was no pressure from external examinations and classes were kept to around 16 or 20 the subject provided many opportunities for the pupil to develop in accordance with his individual talents.

Mixed ability groups were not however considered helpful in preparing pupils for external examinations. As one teacher explained, 'Exams create difficulties. More depth is required for GCE and CSE work and it is difficult to teach a whole mixed group. Teaching is to the median, therefore the able and the less able suffer from lack of attention.' Here the nature of the subject was not seen to be causing problems but the demands exerted by pressures of time affected the way in which the teacher was free to organize subject activities. In an area where work was regarded as 'individually based' and 'child centred', examinations appeared to create considerable difficulties.

Table 6.11: *Teaching methods: technical studies*

Teaching Method	Frequency of Use (N = 24)					
	Very Frequent	Frequent	Sometimes	Very Occasional	Never	All Teachers
Individual learning	6	6	4	1	7	24
Small groups	1	9	5	0	9	24
Large groups	1	5	3	1	14	24
Whole class	12	8	2	0	2	24
More than one class	2	1	3	3	15	24

Twenty-four of the 26 technical studies teachers in the sample were involved with mixed ability groups at the time of the investigation. Their methods of classroom organization appear in Table 6.11 and it is apparent that teachers made greatest and most frequent use of whole class teaching, a method which dominated the work of five of the 24 members of staff interviewed. Individual learning and small group activities followed class teaching in both extent and frequency of use, while less than half of the teachers used large groups or taught more than one class.

Whole class teaching was used for theory work, for issuing instructions and organizing pupils at the start of a lesson and also for short periods during a lesson as the need arose. The emphasis on individual work was strong. In lower forms individual tasks were strictly supervised with the aim of encouraging pupils to work safely on their own so that they would subsequently be able to direct their own progress, once basic skills had been mastered and confidence acquired. A commonly recorded methodology was for the teacher to set a task, solve it theoretically by class teaching and then organize the pupils to solve it individually in a practical way. The more able pupil who finished quickly was encouraged to do a further job involving the process already learned, to improve the article or drawing produced, or to do extra work at home.

Groups were used by 15 of the 24 teachers, and in 12 cases staff intervened in their composition. A pupil's ability and the nature of the work being undertaken were the two prime factors considered, with friendships, deployment of equipment, use of space and class control playing a less important part. Pupil-selected groups were observed to contain a mix of ability in most instances.

Teaching units of more than one class sometimes occurred as a result of timetabling several classes together for technical studies and then dividing pupils among the various subjects offered. A member of staff might teach the boys and girls from two or three different classes in what could be termed an 'option' class. In this subject a group of more than one class did not usually imply a team teaching situation in a large hall, but was more often several teachers working in a series of craft rooms with groups of up to 20 pupils. Two references to team teaching as it is more usually understood, however, were made; in one instance this system had been used for showing films and in the other for a lead lesson for boys of the first and second years followed by work in groups of their own choosing.

viii. *Music*

Almost half of the staff interviewed saw both possibilities and problems for mixed ability teaching; the remainder were divided equally into the two opposing viewpoints – 'Too wide an ability range' at one extreme and 'All can contribute' at the other.

The joy of making music, of participating in a corporate activity, was the central theme of musicians, who felt that every pupil in a mixed ability class could offer something towards practical music making. However, difficulties occurred when teachers introduced theory work, considered to be an integral part of music studies. Differences in the ability of individual pupils to master this new skill resulted in changes in the pattern of the group's progress. One teacher who tried to ensure that all pupils had mastered one point before moving on to the next in the desired 'logical sequence' reported that the brighter children were held up. Basic reading skills were regarded as a prerequisite for music, since teachers expected pupils to be able to read songsheets, instructions and short paragraphs of background material.

In general most teachers of music perceived scope within the subject for contributions from all children in a shared musical experience. Theory and examination work, however, were regarded as generally unsuited to a mixed ability class, as these were seen to impose constraints of time, to restrict course content and to introduce an extraneous element of competition.

Table 6.12: *Teaching methods: music*

Teaching Method	Very Frequent	Frequent	Sometimes	Very Occasional	Never	All Teachers
			Frequency of Use (N = 11)			
Individual learning	0	1	4	2	4	11
Small groups	1	4	4	1	1	11
Large groups	0	3	2	1	5	11
Whole class	9	2	0	0	0	11
More than one class	0	1	4	3	3	11

Music was a subject in which every teacher made frequent or very frequent use of whole class teaching (Table 6.12), which was also the dominant organizational mode for two members of staff. Small groups were used by all but one of the teachers interviewed. Groups of more than one class, individual learning and large groups were all used to some extent by music teachers, but never very frequently.

Class teaching was appropriate for listening to music, for theory work and for singing. Groups were in every case influenced in their structure by the teacher, with musical ability the prime consideration and the nature of the topic the second; teachers were concerned in group work to ensure a mix of musical abilities appropriate to the task and to avoid the creation of one 'poor' group; less attention was given to pupil friendship and classroom control. Groups were used in choral singing, for topic studies such as work on harmony and for instrumental practice. One teacher mentioned that he did not organize this as frequently as he would wish, since there was a lack of small practice rooms. Groups of more than one class were used for singing and for orchestra work.

ix.   Domestic studies

The majority of teachers considered that this subject lent itself to a mixed ability approach in certain respects; only two members of staff were convinced that mixed ability classes were totally inappropriate for domestic studies. In the sample interviewed, the greatest number of teachers were involved with cookery and needlework, a smaller number with child care, health education, home management and nutrition.

Teachers perceived domestic studies as a mainly practical subject which divided readily into smaller units of work in which 'everyone can do something'. The development of individual skills was stressed, and teachers saw needlework in particular as affording considerable opportunity for pupils to progress at a pace suited to their aptitude and ability. Co-operation was encouraged and teachers perceived cookery practicals as providing a particularly suitable environment for the fostering of co-operative endeavour.

Difficulties inherent in the nature of the subject stemmed from the basic division of domestic studies into practical and theoretical aspects. 'Practical' difficulties centred around the very fact – perceived to be advantageous from the pupil's point of view – that progress was made at widely differing rates. In a mixed ability class this feature was exacerbated, presenting a special problem in cookery where it was considered necessary for each child to have a finished product at the end of a practical lesson.

Theoretical difficulties arose in all areas of domestic studies when teachers endeavoured to bring pupils to the same level of understanding at a given time. The constraints of examination syllabuses were seen to intensify these problems in the fourth and fifth years, and several teachers considered that it was necessary 'to stream within the class' if they were to prepare their pupils adequately for examinations. Thus the subject was seen as providing pupils with the opportunity to develop practical skills and to explore theoretical issues but, as one teacher observed, 'theory and practical work in one lesson can cause problems' with a mixed ability group.

Table 6.13: *Teaching methods: domestic studies*

Teaching Methods	Very Frequent	Frequent	Sometimes	Very Occasional	Never	All Teachers
Individual learning	9	3	2	6	4	24
Small groups	2	9	2	0	11	24
Large groups	1	2	2	2	17	24
Whole class	14	6	1	0	3	24
More than one class	0	0	1	6	17	24

Frequency of Use (N = 24)

Domestic studies afforded the teacher a wide range of approaches. All methods of classroom organization were used and the scope offered for the development of individual styles was reflected in the record of dominant teaching methods. For one teacher individual learning dominated classroom activities, for another it was group work and for six staff members whole class teaching was the dominant mode of organization. Class teaching was used by the greatest number of teachers and was also adopted more frequently than any other method. Individual learning followed class teaching in the extent of its use; large and small groups were employed by 15 of the 24 teachers and only seven teachers sometimes encountered groups of more than one class.

As already noted, the two main subjects taught were cookery and needlework.

These subjects revealed different patterns of classroom organization, since as might be expected individual learning dominated in needlework lessons while cookery was more often a group activity. In all domestic subjects, however, a whole class approach formed the basis for theory work, demonstrations and for the issuing of instructions about practical work. Class teaching frequently took place at the start of a lesson when staff explained the work to be done and organized pupils' activities, and near the conclusion of a lesson to supervise clearing up procedures and to go over the main points again. Individual learning was used for both theoretical and practical aspects of domestic studies and work was usually guided by the teacher. Worksheets were rarely used for structuring individual tasks.

Large or small groups were called together as necessary in order that the teacher might explain a point over which certain pupils were experiencing difficulty. The frequency of such groups naturally varied from lesson to lesson, and pupils' ability was the chief deciding factor, linked with the nature of the topic. Three of the teachers let pupils select their own groups and in two cases it was considered that a mix of ability resulted, while in the third a pattern of 'slow tables and fast tables' was created. Groups of more than one class were not taught on a regular basis in domestic studies as specialist rooms were not designed to cope with large numbers of pupils. Occasionally classes were called together to see a film or to listen to a visiting speaker.

x.   *Mathematics*

Mathematics teachers did not generally perceive their subject as well suited to a mixed ability approach. Approximately half of those interviewed considered it totally unsuitable for mixed ability teaching largely because they perceived it as having a logical structure through which pupils must proceed in a prescribed way. It was clear that the majority of mathematics teachers interviewed saw their subject as comprising a given body of knowledge which required an ordered method of exploration. In this context mathematical concepts needed to be learned and practised in a logical sequence, and this presented problems in a mixed ability class. Frequent comments pertaining to the 'laddered', 'structured', 'sequential', 'linear' and 'cumulative' qualities of mathematics indicated the nature of perceptions held by a majority of teachers in the sample.

The greatest difficulty encountered by mathematics teachers

arose from the fact that pupils not only learn at different rates but that they also have different powers of retention. There is 'always the child who can't remember what he did yesterday' and also the 'bright who get put off if not extended'. Thus some teachers had found it virtually impossible to move logically through a series of concepts within a mathematical topic with the whole class. An illustrative comment was that with 'kids at different levels a single approach is not viable and mathematics should be taught individually'.

Some advantages were perceived as accruing from mixed ability teaching in the first year, where pupils' mathematical backgrounds were largely unknown. As the subject was commonly regarded as sequential and 'building on past knowledge' it was considered by a number of teachers that mixed ability grouping in year one (and in some cases in year two) facilitated mathematical learning in this transitional phase and overcame differences in pupils' previous mathematical experience. By the third year, however, most teachers felt that the difference in pupils' capacities to cope with specific concepts made mixed ability mathematics very difficult to teach. The examination system was seen to influence work in the upper school, but the nature of the subject rather than the presence of examinations appeared to be the major force behind the wish to stream or to set.

A few teachers questioned the linear aspects of the subject and maintained that topic work was both feasible and desirable. Once the topic had been analysed and broken down into units it was possible for pupils to work their way through at their own pace. Basic skills were necessary, but a prescribed sequence of work in mathematics was not deemed essential. The degree to which teachers considered that mathematics could be divided into topics appeared to be a key factor influencing their perceptions of the success of the strategies selected for mixed ability teaching.

Forty-three of the 66 teachers of mathematics interviewed were involved with mixed ability groups at the time of the research (Table 6.14). Information on teaching methods indicated that mathematics and commercial studies were the only subjects in which individual learning was used as frequently as class teaching. Table 6.14 indicates that in mathematics, class teaching was used by all but five teachers and individual learning by all but six, with the latter having the highest incidence of very frequent use. Groups were used by 22 of the 43 teachers and team teaching methods by only six.

Table 6.14: *Teaching methods: mathematics*

Teaching methods	Frequency of Use (N = 43) Very Frequent	Frequent	Sometimes	Very Occasional	Never	All Teachers
Individual learning	21	9	4	3	6	43
Small groups	6	2	7	5	23	43
Large groups	1	2	6	4	30	43
Whole class	19	10	6	3	5	43
More than one class	0	2	1	3	37	43

Class teaching was commonly used to introduce a new topic, for revision exercises, for giving information and instructions at the start of a lesson and for short periods during a lesson as pupil needs dictated. One teacher stressed the importance of maintaining an awareness of pupils' individual capabilities in this situation and explained the necessity of having 'different expectations of each pupil' within the class. Class teaching dominated the work of six mathematics staff.

Four-fifths of the teachers interviewed expressed concern about devising ways in which pupils' needs could be met on an individual basis within a mixed ability class. Bearing in mind both the logical nature of mathematics and also the pupils' widely differing powers of learning and retention, many staff used independent schemes of work and this approach dominated in the work of three teachers. It was considered possible to design workcards and worksheets which allowed for widely differing rates of progress. For example, one pupil might be directed by the teacher to use specific cards so that basic points only were covered, another, known to be a quick and able worker, could be directed towards extension exercises by means of asterisked questions or by the use of another card containing more advanced work. This system was seen to provide sufficient flexibility for all pupils to progress according to their particular strengths or weaknesses, but required that the teacher knew pupils individually so that work of an appropriate level might be assigned. An important advantage of this approach was that one child did not hold up the entire class as in a more formal teaching situation, and the teacher, released from the blackboard zone, was free to move round the class to assist those in difficulty. Teachers also maintained that the use of worksheets spaced out claims on their time in class, since all pupils did not encounter the same problem at once. One ingenious mathematics teacher devised a simple but effective scheme to ensure that all pupils who required attention had an equal chance of receiving it and that the pattern of such requests was monitored. When a pupil needed assistance, he wrote his name on a piece of paper on the teacher's desk and then returned to his seat to attempt another section of work or to revise work already covered. The teacher, by referring to this paper, could see not only who needed help most urgently, but also, from the pattern of names at the lesson end, who was experiencing particular problems in mathematics. This provided a written record of immense use in identifying the nature of a problem and in noting pupils' progress and also did away with the teacher's nightmare – a queue of anxious but time-wasting pupils which can quickly turn a serious working atmosphere into one far less conducive to study. The School Mathematics Project materials were widely used as the basis for individual learning programmes in mixed ability mathematics classes.

Close links between class teaching and individual learning in mathematics were apparent in many cases and it is not surprising that their recorded patterns of classroom use were similar. The degree to which these two methods were interwoven is illustrated by one teacher who taught the whole class for a short time and then divided the blackboard into three sections, so that all pupils would work through the first section, some would tackle the second and a few would attempt the third. Another teacher found that 'switching from class teaching to individual learning' and vice versa reduced personal stress as he was no longer the focus of attention throughout the lesson.

Groups were used by approximately half of the teachers interviewed. Small groups were set up for revision, for mathematical games (directed by workcards) and for pupils who wished to explore a specific topic or as one teacher explained 'to delve into a problem'. Both large and small groups were created on an *ad hoc* basis for problem solving with the teacher's assistance as the need arose. In 16 out of the 22 cases in which groups were used teachers influenced group structure, with pupils' ability the main consideration; friendship, the nature of the topic and classroom control received less frequent attention. Teachers structured groups with a particular aim in mind; a mix was contrived for a mathematical game and a restricted range was sought for problem solving discussions. One teacher considered it essential for the teacher to select pupils on an ability basis for all types of group work.

Team teaching when it occurred was generally used to introduce a new topic. Groups of more than one class were not regarded as particularly appropriate for work in mathematics and only six teachers were involved in team teaching, none of them very frequently.

From the strategies outlined it is clear that a necessary prerequisite for mixed ability teaching is a plentiful supply of appropriately-designed worksheets and workcards and preferably the services of a reliable reprographics unit. Over a third of staff considered that mixed ability teaching had increased the need for resource materials, a need which was being met in different ways with varying degrees of claimed success. Some teachers were adapting existing materials (both personal and published), others were making their own resources as required and five were working together designing and producing materials for departmental use. The production of teaching materials and the preparation of lessons is always time-consuming; with the introduction of mixed ability groupings, many mathematics teachers reported that this time increased. Of all subject teachers who noted an increase in preparation and marking time, mathematics teachers were proportionally the most strongly represented group – approximately half, as compared with two-fifths of English and non-integrated humanities staff. The most helpful solution was seen to be the sharing of resources and their production, while pupil marking of test items also alleviated the load placed on the individual teacher.

It is clear that in mixed ability mathematics teacher-directed work from a class text was not considered a feasible approach and many teachers had undertaken a restructuring of courses and prepared banks of resources the use of which necessitated a change in the traditional teaching role. Some staff had adapted to these changes, others were still searching for suitable strategies and for ways of meeting the need for appropriate materials. Only 14 per cent of mathematics teachers considered their subject wholly suitable for a mixed ability approach and after the first and second year difficulties with abstract concepts and the wide differences in the rates of pupils' progress were found hard to contain; it was therefore generally considered that the needs of individual pupils could best be met within a setted or streamed class from the third year onwards.

xi. *Commerce*

There were very few commerce teachers in the sample and the fact that only one of the seven interviewed saw commerce as wholly suitable for a mixed ability approach explains why in the present discussion it is ranked between mathematics and modern languages in terms of low positive response (v Table 6.1). In fact the remaining six commerce teachers saw their subject as suited to mixed ability teaching in some respects and serious problems appeared to be few. Pupils were motivated to work when they could 'see some relevance to their own life' and in commercial studies this link was clear. Resources were seen as suitable for both streamed and unstreamed groups since the subject was concerned with the development of individual skills. Individual work was the keynote and typing in particular was perceived as lending itself equally readily to a streamed and mixed ability class. Some teacher difficulties were mentioned in the early stages when pupils were being taught the basic skills, but once this stage was past it was accepted, indeed expected, that pupils would progress at widely differing rates.

Table 6.15: *Teaching methods: commercial studies*

Teaching Method	Very Frequent	Frequent	Sometimes	Very Occasional	Never	All Teachers
			Frequency of Use (N = 6)			
Individual learning	3	3	0	0	0	6
Small groups	0	1	2	0	3	6
Large groups	0	1	1	1	3	6
Whole class	4	1	1	0	0	6
More than one class	0	0	0	0	6	6

Six of the seven commercial studies teachers interviewed were teaching mixed ability groups. All six used whole class teaching and individual learning techniques, four used groups and none ever taught more than one class. No teaching method was dominant but individual learning and class teaching were used frequently or very frequently by all but one of the teachers interviewed.

Few comments were made on teaching styles. Individual work included skills practice and assignment tasks while class teaching was commonly used for instruction in basic techniques. Three of the four teachers employing groups influenced their structure in order to encourage pupils to help each other with specific points of difficulty, hence the chief factors they considered were pupil ability and the nature of the topic. One member of staff who directed the more able pupils towards helping the slower workers found this a helpful strategy as the able came to realize the difficulties in the subject and to appreciate the nature of the teacher's task; co-operation was also seen to aid the pupils' social development.

xii.   Modern Languages

Teachers of modern languages, traditionally a subject area in which the introduction of heterogeneous grouping has been resisted, exhibited predictable responses in that the majority considered that mixed ability language work was neither desirable nor feasible.

The few teachers who perceived mixed ability grouping in French or German to be a workable mode of organization considered that it should be restricted to years one and two where most work was oral and considerable use could be made of audio visual material. Social interaction and communication of the spoken language were two objectives which teachers felt it possible to realize in a mixed ability class. Audio visual stimulus material was considered to provide the opportunity for each child to achieve a degree of personal success according to his aptitudes and efforts.

When the stated objectives were those of examination success, however, modern languages posed all the expected problems of a subject which is perceived as 'highly structured', 'cumulative', 'laddered', 'sequential' and relying on the acquisition and retention of language skills. As one teacher explained, the feasibility of mixed ability teaching 'depends on the objectives of language teaching'. In the first year, it was considered that a major objective was 'to understand and communicate the spoken language' and in this context audio visual methods were considered 'good for mixed ability classes' where 'all can contribute' and 'vital social interaction' was perceived to take place. But with spoken French and German the move from simple sentences into more complex structures was perceived as one which not all pupils were ready to make at the same time. In a teacher-centred subject this was seen to present insoluble problems: 'The very slow need repetition when the fairly fast are ready to move on.' Sometimes pupils proficient in the language were asked to assist pupils who were experiencing difficulties, but teachers viewed this as an expedient rather than a solution to the problem.

Audio visual work was considered only part of an approach to the study of a foreign language and the move from the spoken to the written word had to be made at some stage during the first year. The precision required of pupils in written work was seen to present similar problems of pace. Wide individual differences in pupils' ability to grasp grammatical points, to concentrate on a given topic or to retain what they had learned did not permit the class to progress as a whole. Modern language work was regarded as demanding too disciplined an approach from some pupils – particularly those poor at English. One teacher commented that 'pupils operate at different levels so you lose the lower end and the interest of the more able . . .written work is problematical as the less able cannot grasp the grammatical content. Is language worth teaching if it is watered down?'

Another teacher explained that there was little scope in language for topic work or original project work as the bulk of modern language teaching centred around a core of spoken and written linguistic material which required mastery by the pupil in a logical sequence. A class with a wide range of ability was perceived to militate against this logical progression, presenting insuperable problems for the teacher of modern languages. Modern language teachers faced with a mixed ability class were clearly torn between the requirements of a precise linguistic discipline and the demands of a group of children whose abilities, aptitudes and inclinations were widely varying.

A few teachers saw possibilities for the teaching of modern languages in mixed ability classes. With a plentiful supply of resources these teachers considered that work could be structured for each pupil according to his needs and that with 'a moving scale of expectations' it was possible to record progress on an individual basis. This was considered feasible as long as the class was free from the pressures of examinations. French studies and European studies with a reduced linguistic content reflected an attempt made by some schools to provide courses for those pupils who were unsuited for an academic language course. Considerable development, however, was seen as necessary in order to create a firm structure for such courses and remove them from an uneasy limbo between languages and the humanities.

Table 6.16:   *Teaching methods: modern languages*

Teaching method	Frequency of Use (N = 40)					
	Very Frequent	Frequent	Sometimes	Very Occasional	Never	All Teachers
Individual learning	2	6	2	7	23	40
Small groups	1	5	11	9	14	40
Large groups	1	7	5	4	23	40
Whole class	35	5	0	0	0	40
More than one class	0	0	1	4	35	40

Forty of the 55 language teachers in the sample taught mixed ability classes. Every teacher of such classes taught the class as a whole, small groups were used by 26, while individual learning and large groups were each used by 17 teachers. Only five members of staff were involved at any stage with groups of more than one class (Table 6.16).

All modern linguists made frequent or very frequent use of whole class teaching, and for 12 teachers this was the dominant organizational mode. Emphasis on the spoken word in the early stages of language learning had resulted in a teacher-centred situation to which individual staff could see little alternative. Audio visual techniques are an integral part of language courses, but again these rely on the teacher for activation. The oral exchange between pupil and teacher was seen as the core of all language work and one teacher summarized the feelings of many with the statement that 'in modern languages the teacher is the only authority in the classroom'.

Clearly, teachers were concerned that the needs of all pupils in a mixed ability class should be met but proffered 'solutions' were few. Fewer than half of the teachers who expressed conern over the more able pupils could see any way of providing for their needs in an unstreamed class. However, language 'readers' of an appropriate degree of difficulty were considered helpful in providing work at a more advanced level, while participation in drama and individual work – preferably in a language laboratory – were also seen as ways of 'extending' the linguistically more able pupil. With one class the teacher had devised a worksheet on which the able worked through every question, the pupil of average ability did alternate questions and the less able pupil attempted 'as much as possible'.

The nature of solutions put forward for use with less able pupils differed little from those designed for the more able, namely readers, drama work, individual oral work using tapes and with the teacher. Two additional methods were the use of simple workcards and help from the more able pupils in class. One teacher, aware of certain pupils' lack of concentration, divided the class into groups. Oral work took place in 'short bursts' and it was considered essential to have a variety of activities – acting, drawing, reading, writing – in order to maintain the interest of all pupils throughout the lesson. Another member of staff was planning a series of graded worksheets on specific topics (e.g. telling the time) as he considered there was a need for language resources which were simple and self-contained and on which pupils could work for short periods.

Groups were used by 29 of the 40 modern linguists and in 23 cases teachers influenced group structure, taking pupil ability and the nature of the topic into account more frequently than friendship ties or disciplinary factors. Teachers stressed the importance of achieving a mix of ability for drama groups and role-play but considered a restricted range of ability to be more appropriate where pupils were working together on a specific topic or task. Small groups were used for drama, role-play, 'background' studies to the spoken language and for French or German conversation with a foreign assistant.

Individual learning methods in modern languages took the form of teacher-pupil interaction on a one to one basis, laboratory work and, to a lesser extent, worksheet-guided tasks. Staff considered it particularly important to structure work so that each child could achieve something, however simple, and in this context it was important to recognize effort. The constraint most frequently expressed by teachers was a lack of time for preparation of materials.

Groups of more than one class were organized periodically by five of the teachers interviewed. Films and drama were the two situations considered suitable for this approach.

No strategies were put forward by modern language teachers which purported to 'solve' the problem of teaching pupils in a mixed ability class; instead, teachers described methods which they had found helpful in coping with the demands made by individual pupils who were progressing at different rates in the subject; such differences in pace were highlighted by the introduction of written grammar and intensified by the passing of time.

xiii.   Teachers with no main subject
There were 10 teachers who taught more than one subject and who therefore were not allocated a main subject. Of these, six worked in the humanities, teaching between them English, religious education, environmental studies, inter-disciplinary enquiry, history, geography and general studies. All except one considered their subject area well suited to a mixed ability approach, following the response pattern set by teachers for whom humanities was a main subject. The remaining four teachers held varying opinions. One considered careers education unsuited to mixed ability teaching, another taught mathematics, physics, biology and humanities and considered all four subjects unsuitable for teaching to mixed ability classes. The member of staff who taught English and mathematics considered the former suitable and the latter unsuitable, while the fourth teacher, involved with mathematics and technical drawing, considered that both subjects lent themselves in some respects to a mixed ability organization.

4.   Discussion
It is apparent from the evidence cited in this chapter that not only were lessons organized in a wide variety of ways but also that subjects were seen as differing considerably in their nature; in consequence some were perceived as generally suitable for a mixed ability approach and others regarded as largely unsuitable. The humanities, for example, were commonly viewed as providing excellent opportunities for mixed ability work, while modern languages and mathematics were considered to present problems which were regarded as insuperable by many of those who taught mixed ability classes. What makes a subject particularly well suited

to a mixed ability approach? Why are some subjects regarded as unsuitable for teaching to mixed ability classes?

The absence of clear-cut criteria for correctness and the acceptability of a range of differing responses rather than a single 'right' answer appear as key factors affecting the perceived suitability of a subject for mixed ability teaching. The opportunity afforded for individual contributions in class discussion, drama and role play in the humanities and in English was seen as a valuable way of involving all pupils in the lesson and enabling them to learn from one another. In aesthetic subjects and in physical education where one of the principal aims was to develop a pupil's individual aptitude in the subject, teachers similarly encountered relatively few problems. Differing rates of progress were not considered a serious difficulty in domestic and technical studies in the early years of secondary school and, again, much of the work in these subjects involved the pupil in individual tasks.

More reservations existed among scientists, who felt that beyond the first or second year, mixed ability classes presented some problems as pupils were not all able to grasp the concepts involved. However, teachers considered that science presented many opportunities for individual contributions, provided that it was accepted that pupils engaged in the same activity would exhibit varying degrees of competence.

Mathematicians were divided – those who favoured an individual, resource-based topic approach, saw considerable opportunity in this subject for a pupil to work at his own pace, but those who saw the subject as sequential, tended also to require the class to proceed together through a series of prescribed steps and did not consider the subject suited to a mixed ability form of organization.

Of any group of subject teachers, modern linguists saw the fewest possibilities in their discipline for mixed ability teaching. There was, however, some scope for individual contributions to be made in oral work during the first year, when it was considered important to build up pupils' confidence in the spoken language and to encourage all to join in classwork with some degree of personal success. Almost nine out of ten of those interviewed, however, considered mixed ability groups to be totally unsuitable for teaching modern languages or had serious reservations about them.

In the foregoing paragraphs there is evidence to suggest that an important factor which affects how appropriate a subject is for mixed ability teaching is its perceived structure. Where, for example, a discipline was seen to require pupils to work through a specific body of knowledge in a prescribed logical sequence, the problems presented by a class with a wide range of ability were often considered insuperable. Teachers of mathematics, physics and modern languages stressed this point frequently, historians and geographers less often. Music teachers encountered problems when theory work was introduced. Subjects with prescribed structures appeared to present particular difficulties in mixed ability classes when the whole class teaching approach was adopted.

In contrast, the ease with which English, the humanities, art, craft, general science and domestic studies permitted division into a number of relatively independent themes or topics facilitated mixed ability teaching in these subjects. For example, topic work in general science was perceived as suitable for mixed ability classes whereas physics as a scientific discipline was not. Mathematics provides a further interesting case; those teachers who considered the subject 'logical' and 'sequential' saw few possibilities for mixed ability work, but staff who saw it as a series of topics which readily permitted division into smaller units regarded it as well-suited to mixed ability classes, at least in the first year of secondary school.

A further important consideration is the role of the teacher in the classroom. When the teacher was perceived as the central or major resource of the classroom, fewer possibilities were seen for mixed ability teaching than in subjects where other resources such as worksheets, workbooks, pamphlets, films, tapes, etc. were available. The teaching of modern languages, where class teaching was used extensively, illustrates this point well; in no other subject did almost one-third of the staff employ class teaching as the dominant organizational mode. On the other hand, the humanities subjects, including English, stand out as a group in which a considerable variety of resource materials was seen to enhance any teaching situation. Stress was placed by staff on the importance of the stimulus afforded by a number of different resources and the flexibility of teaching approach which these made possible. In mathematics, those teachers who considered the subject suitable for a mixed ability approach considered the existence of a bank of resource materials a necessary prerequisite.

Several other factors appear to determine how far a subject is seen to lend itself to a mixed ability approach. The need for pupils to become familiar with a technical vocabularly, involving the under-standing of concepts of increasing generality and abstractness as well as the learning of labels, presented particular difficulties in subjects such as physics and geography. Also, the extent to which examination pressures were felt at any particular stage by teachers determined their perceptions of the suitability of mixed ability work in a number of subjects. In English, history, geography, general science, music, domestic and technical studies, for example, where relatively few problems were reported in the early secondary years, teachers' awareness of examination requirements led them to reject mixed grouping when the need to prepare for these became appar-ent. Related to this, the degree to which teachers viewed their subject as a means of achieving other than strictly academic out-comes also appeared to affect their perceptions of its suitability for teaching to mixed ability classes.

The teachers' evidence summarized in the preceding paragraphs points to a series of questions which might be asked about a subject at any stage where mixed ability teaching is being considered:

(a) Is the subject such that a range of individual responses at a variety of levels rather than 'set' answers are acceptable?

(b) Is the subject viewed as being so structured that it requires the acquisition of a specific body of knowledge in a prescribed sequence?

(c) How readily can the subject be divided into relatively discrete topics or themes? How far can work be organized so that a pupil can proceed independently at his own pace?

(d) How far can a variety of activities usefully be employed to mediate knowledge and skills?

(e) How far is it feasible to deploy resources other than the teacher; are such resources available?

(f) How far is progress in the subject dependent on the mastery of a technical vocabulary and of a range of complex concepts?

(g) How important is the achievement of outcomes other than those which might be described as strictly academic in the teaching of the subject?

(h) To what extent do examination requirements impinge on the teaching of the subject at various stages?

This chapter has also reviewed the teaching approaches and methods of classroom organization employed by teachers in differ-ent subject areas. The evidence broadly confirms the comments in

Chapter Five which indicated a widespread use of class teaching; indeed, only in mathematics and commerce did any other teaching mode – in these cases individualized work – occur as frequently. Further, for 54 teachers classroom teaching was their dominant teaching mode as we have defined it. There is clearly a danger of whole class teaching becoming the bogey of those who write and talk about mixed ability work. It is apparent from the preceding pages that many teachers were using it as but one part of a battery of teaching strategies, to introduce and end lessons or to explain points of general interest or concern. What is important is that teachers are able to select the most effective strategy for the task in hand and there will be occasions when this is whole class teaching. It is evident, however, from comments reported in this and the preceding chapter that to attempt to teach a heterogeneous group of pupils in this way in inappropriate circumstances can present formidable problems.

Chapter Seven

Pointers

'It is evident that all schools must group their pupils for social, academic and pastoral purposes. In making these decisions schools have to attempt to reconcile objectives which, in some ways, may appear to be conflicting. For example, for some purposes groups of varied abilities may be suitable while for others more homogeneous groupings may be more appropriate. It is clear that there is no one best way of organizing pupils for all purposes and that individual schools adopt a variety of practices' (DES, 1979).

In the first chapter of this report we referred to the results of a survey carried out in 1975 of the grouping practices used in comprehensive schools. A further survey in the academic year 1979–80 makes it possible to compare the situation then and now (Table 7.1). Although there has been some decrease in the percentage of schools employing mixed ability groups as the dominant mode of organizing pupils for teaching purposes in the second and third years of their secondary education, the striking fact to emerge from these two enquiries is the remarkable degree of consistency in the incidence of mixed ability grouping over a five-year period during which it has been vigorously debated. Very little difference also has occurred in the relatively small proportion of schools using streaming as their means of organizing teaching groups in 1980 as compared with 1975. Banding, however, which is sometimes viewed as a half-way house between a policy of rigid streaming on the one hand and of groups of heterogeneous ability on the other, is much less common now than in 1975; nevertheless it still approximates to the incidence of mixed ability grouping in the second year and considerably surpasses it in the third. Of major interest in the figures presented in Table 7.1, however, is first the increase, particularly in the second and third years, of schools using setting as their main method of grouping pupils, and second, of schools using a combination of different grouping practices to the extent that they were unable to identify any mode of grouping as dominant. Five years ago no school was unable to identify a dominant mode in any of the first three years of secondary education. What, then, is emerging is a trend towards greater variety and flexibility, a recognition perhaps in terms of school practice of the point made in the quotation which opens this chapter that there is no one best way of organizing pupils for all purposes.

It has been argued that the goal of evaluation studies should be the 'reduction of uncertainties' about the consequences of alternative courses of action (Cronbach, 1978). Yet it is apparent from the evidence cited in the preceding chapters that there are both substantial benefits and considerable difficulties associated with mixed ability grouping and that these vary among subjects, year groups, individual schools and teachers. It is little wonder that the results of previous researches into mixed ability grouping have been conflicting, for the one certainty that emerges from our study is that any attempt to make statements in general terms supporting or condemning it are demonstrably naïve. The great majority of practitioners – heads and assistant teachers drawn from widely varying schools – who gave the project the benefit of their comment will not be surprised at this conclusion. That much of the public debate on grouping practices has been characterized by extreme statements reflects the association of educational issues in this instance with deeply-felt social and political commitments.

How has this report, then, contributed to that 'reduction of uncertainties' which Cronbach considers an essential characteristic of evaluative research? Given that what one teacher in one set of circumstances perceives as advantageous may be perceived by another in different circumstances as disadvantageous, the most fruitful approach would appear to lie in trying to identify those contexts which generally appear to facilitate or constrain mixed ability teaching. The evidence reported in the preceding chapters is rich in pointers and, by way of summary, some of those will now be considered.

First, there are strong indications (v Chapter Three) that the way

Table 7.1: *Schools' grouping arrangements in 1975 and 1980 in the first three years of secondary education*

	(Percentage schools) Year Group		
	First	Second	Third
Grouping Arrangement	%	%	%
Mixed Ability Groups			
1975	55	37	25
1980	55	32	18
Streams			
1975	6	9	12
1980	9	11	12
Bands			
1975	37	48	54
1980	23	30	31
Sets/Other			
1975	2	5	9
1980	5	15	23
No dominant grouping arrangement			
1975	—	—	—
1980	7	11	16
Number of schools sampled			
1975	854	906	969
1980	491	529	573

in which mixed ability teaching is introduced to a school and, in particular, the nature and extent of the consultation which takes place, may be a factor of major importance in its subsequent operation. This may indeed be true for any innovation. In over two-thirds of the schools studied the initiative in introducing mixed ability grouping came from the head and the methods employed have been broadly classified as 'directive'. The role of the head in initiating change in his school has long been a matter for discussion. Owen (1970) drew attention to the importance of the head in such innovation and Hoyle (1969) observed that 'the willingness of a school to institutionalize curriculum development is very much dependent upon the manner in which the head teacher performs his leadership role'. Hughes (1972) found wide differences among heads in their perceptions of the part they played, or should play, in promoting change. Referring to the introduction of mixed ability teaching, he quotes comments which echo some of those reported in Chapter Three: 'I *told* staff rather than consulted them. I know if I had consulted them they would have been against it.' He reports other comments relating to innovation in general: 'That is what the head is there for'; 'the majority of staff need some prodding'; 'staff are generally very conservative; it is mainly the head who attends courses'; 'the head must be the catalytic agent if the heads of department are barren of ideas'.

The tension between the head as initiator and the staff as professionals competent to judge what is appropriate for their teaching is well exemplified in documents produced some years ago by the National Union of Teachers, on the one hand, and the Headmasters' Association on the other:

> ... 'We recommend as an interim measure that the Union immediately declares it should be the right of all members of staff to be consulted on matters affecting the school in general and their own work in particular, and that it should be obligatory for head teachers to make satisfactory arrangements within their schools for such consultation' (NUT (1972). *The Right of Teachers to Consultation.* A declaration by the Executive of the NUT).

> '... control could easily fall into the hands of an unrepresentative group. This might be a reactionary band who would oppose all change: it might equally well in some schools be an idealistic and enthusiastic group determined to make revolutionary changes but lacking the experience to see either the difficulties which would arise or the need for careful preparation. We would add that those keenest to acquire power are not necessarily those whose judgement commands our greatest respect' (Headmasters' Association (1972). *The Government of Schools.*)

The 'revolutionary change' in the case of mixed ability teaching came as we have noted, not usually from an 'idealistic and enthusiastic group' but from the head himself. Whilst it is not within the scope of this discussion to comment in general terms on the role of the head as innovator, it is apparent in the case of mixed ability teaching that this innovation requires far-reaching changes not only in teaching approaches but also in the role of teacher in the

classroom and in the ways he relates to his colleagues. The concern
of heads that such changes had in many cases not occurred is
reported in Chapter Three; evidence cited in Chapters Five and Six
suggests a widespread use of the whole class approach to mixed
ability teaching, an emphasis on 'teaching to the middle' and a
tendency among teachers to see themselves as functioning in isolation from their colleagues – even in some cases from those within
the same department. Whilst factors other than the mode of introduction are certainly pertinent here, it is unlikely that changes in
teaching style and relationships as profound as those which appear
to be required in mixed ability teaching can be effected without
extensive consultation, discussion, persuasion and support.

It may be particularly pertinent at the present time that schools
develop adequate mechanisms for such consultation, for there are
far-reaching changes affecting the education service which may
mean that some schools and teachers virtually have mixed ability
teaching 'thrust upon them' – and it is important that teachers
understand fully the reasons for this and also any alternatives open
to those who manage schools. Briault and Smith (1980a), reporting
on a study of 20 schools with falling rolls, noted reductions in the
average number of teaching groups per subject in all but four
schools. A large part in each reduction was the drop in the number
of teaching groups in compulsory subjects following a fall in roll, but
there was also a drop in the number of groups in optional subjects,
with the result that fewer teaching groups were able to have
separate examination objectives. The authors comment: 'It is true
that many schools have moved towards more mixed ability teaching, particularly for younger pupils . . . But this is a different matter
from its being enforced by the smallness of the number of pupils in
the fourth and fifth year teaching groups for this or that subject. The
practicability of providing adequately for older pupils in mixed
ability groups must remain questionable, at least while many examination syllabuses remain different for pupils of different levels of
ability.' In the second part of their report Briault and Smith (1980b)
express the view that it may be as important for schools 'to assess the
effect upon older pupils in the main school, especially at either end
of the ability scale, of the widening range of ability in some teaching
groups in optional subjects, as it is to consider the effect of a
contraction in the range of optional subjects available to them'.

Providing teachers with the kind of help they need in adapting and developing their current approaches to meet a new teaching situation is not an easy task. A factor which schools introducing mixed ability teaching might well consider is the degree of knowledge and expertise available in their localities whether this be among advisers, in colleges or departments of education or in neighbouring schools. The heads and teachers who took part in our study were widely critical of the capacity of the first two of these – the advisers and staffs of colleges – to give assistance in view of their many commitments, lack of experience in, and in some cases hostility to, mixed ability teaching. Whilst teachers in nearly a third of the schools were able to attend courses organized by their local authorities, by DES/ATO, teacher and subject associations, many schools were forced to draw upon their own resources and organize courses themselves, either on a departmental or whole-school basis. Altogether nearly 40 per cent of the teachers interviewed had taken part in some form of in-service course, but criticisms of such courses on grounds of lack of relevance and lack of sophistication were widespread and no differences were found in attitudes towards mixed ability teaching between those who had attended such courses and those who had not. Further, in the area where attitudes to mixed ability teaching were least favourable, a relatively extensive programme of in-service courses had apparently done little to mitigate teachers' hostility or modify their practice. In contrast, those teachers (32 per cent) whose pre-service training had contained elements on the teaching of unstreamed groups tended to identify advantages in mixed ability teaching more readily than other teachers. They, too, however were critical of the content and methods employed in such elements and it may well be, as noted earlier, that their more favourable attitudes reflect factors other than their training experiences. In short, whilst a substantial proportion – nearly two-thirds – of teachers involved with mixed ability classes had received some form of pre- or in-service training concerned with teaching such classes, relatively few were able to report that such training had been of practical assistance in their subsequent teaching.

In view of the extent to which schools apparently have to support themselves in developing the skills and resources for mixed ability teaching, factors of critical importance are the abilities, attitudes, and experiences of the teaching staff. Particular problems have been noted (Chapter Three) when mixed ability grouping is introduced in newly-amalgamated schools at the time of comprehensive reorganization, where teachers with sometimes widely-varying attitudes and objectives meet children of an ability level not previously encountered. In these and in other schools it seems that previous experience in terms of the ability groups taught may be a major factor associated with how teachers view mixed ability work. Those teachers in our sample who had previously taught in comprehensive schools and had thereby encountered a relatively wide range of ability were more likely to see advantages in mixed ability groups than their colleagues. Those whose only previous experience had been in selective schools, on the other hand, were least likely to consider their subjects suitable for a mixed ability approach. Length of teaching experience also emerged as being significantly associated with teachers' perceptions of mixed ability teaching. Teachers with ten or more years' experience were markedly less favourably disposed towards it than their less experienced colleagues, and Chapter Three documents the particular problems which may be encountered when mixed ability teaching is imposed in schools with a large proportion of these more experienced staff at a time of very low staff turnover.

Of considerable interest is the association found between the amount of time spent on mixed ability teaching and teachers' perceptions of its possibilities. Sixty-three per cent of teachers who spent all their teaching time with mixed ability groups considered their subjects to lend themselves to mixed work as compared with 36 per cent of those who spent half or less of their time with such groups. Interpretation here is not easy; it may be that increased exposure to the new system enables or compels teachers to acquire skills appropriate to it; on the other hand those already disposed towards mixed ability teaching may be given, or themselves seek, a greater amount of work with mixed groups. It is not, however, unreasonable to suppose that the development and trial of new approaches and resources requires that teachers have enough experience of mixed ability groups to enable them to diagnose needs and difficulties and develop ways of meeting them. There may also be a tendency for too little exposure to mixed groups to encourage inactivity as regards developing new approaches, as was indicated by a modern languages teacher teaching a first year mixed ability group who commented that 'you can put up with anything if it's only for one year'. Heads of department were generally less involved with mixed ability groups than other staff, particularly after the early years (Chapter Two).

Teachers' perceptions of the nature of their subject discipline appear to be associated with their views concerning its suitability for a mixed ability approach, and our evidence suggests that heads and heads of department seeking to introduce mixed ability teaching might find advantage in exploring these. Table 6.1 provides a useful indication of those areas of the curriculum in which teachers encounter difficulties. Those teaching English, the humanities, and aesthetic subjects had relatively few reservations concerning the suitability of these subjects for mixed ability work in the early years of secondary education at least; a greater degree of ambivalence occurred among teachers of science, music, technical and domestic studies whilst a large number of the teachers of mathematics (47 per cent) and modern languages (56 per cent) considered their subject unsuitable for teaching to classes with a wide range of ability. A number of factors were identified as being associated with the extent to which teachers considered mixed ability work to be feasible in their subjects; these included how far they perceived their discipline as having a sequential structure as opposed to being readily divisible into a number of loosely-related themes or topics; the extent to which a variety of responses could be accepted; the degree to which progress depended on the mastery of a technical vocabulary and complex conceptual structures, and the feasibility of using resources other than the teacher. The stage at which teachers perceived the demands of the external examination system to exert pressure was also a crucial factor and led in many instances to the abandoning of mixed ability groups in the fourth and fifth years. It was apparent that teachers varied widely in their views of the nature of their subjects; not all mathematicians saw their subject as linear and sequential, and some teachers of the humanities had quite as much to say about their subjects having a logical structure and requiring the mastery of a series of concepts as, say, some scientists. Views concerning the essential characteristics of a discipline are likely to have been acquired over a long period of time and may not readily be susceptible to change. Instances are quoted in Chapter Five of teachers who reported that the introduction of mixed ability teaching had led them to a radical re-think of the nature of their subject. Others were clearly unwilling, unable or unaware of a need to do so. The material presented in Chapter Six, divided as it is into subject areas, may prove helpful to schools and departments as a basis for the examination of their perceptions of the essential features of the various areas of the curriculum.

It seems from our evidence that any such examination will take place in the lunch hour or after school. Only four of the schools studied made curricular time available for departmental discussion although the need for such provision was widely expressed. The pressures on the timetable and the difficulties of identifying and agreeing priorities within it have long exercised those responsible for the management of schools; solutions are, without doubt, hard to find. It is, however, likely that many teachers will be unable effectively to develop new resources and strategies and ways of relating to each other unless time is made available for them to do so.

There are indications in Chapter Three of other ways in which school organization may respond to the needs of teachers involved with teaching mixed ability groups. A number of schools, for example, had found it necessary to review the length of teaching periods, bearing in mind the varying requirements of different subjects and the need to achieve balance between frequency of contact on the one hand and teaching units sufficiently long to make resource-based methods feasible on the other. About half the schools had moved to a blocked timetable to facilitate departments in sharing teaching expertise and resources and also, in some cases, to enable them to group pupils as they wished. Mixed ability teaching was also seen to be facilitated by certain changes in the deployment of the school plant; the establishment of suites of rooms for departments which included a departmental resource centre was widely regarded as a necessary development; centralized resource centres, however, received little support. Adequate reprographic facilities were identified as a necessary prerequisite for mixed ability work in all schools, although only a few had been able to allocate the necessary space for these and acquire a range of equipment; similarly only a few had found means of appointing technicians or re-training existing staff for the production and management of resources. In consequence, the difficulty of producing quality materials in quantity was cited by heads as a major constraint.

Large classes were considered to increase the difficulties of mixed ability work; these were, however, generally accepted as an inevitable fact of life. Few heads or teachers made comments which indicated that they considered the staff contact ratio as defined by Briault and Smith (1980b) to be within the schools' power to change, and the question which they pose in relation to falling rolls in secondary schools may also be pertinent here. 'How far', they ask, 'is the balance between the timetabled teaching required to provide the intended curriculum and the non-timetabled time (required for administration, pastoral care, remedial help for individual pupils, cover for absent teachers, consultation, lesson preparation and marking) the result of a properly considered re-evaluation of priorities and objectives in a changing situation?' Such changes as were found in the organization and deployment of staff associated with the introduction of mixed ability teaching commonly related to changes in pastoral structure designed to bring pastoral and teaching units together, or, in a few instances, to concurrent moves towards the integration of subject disciplines. Such integration was however rarely viewed as a necessary accompaniment to mixed ability teaching and indeed was reported as presenting a number of problems (Chapter Three).

The discussion in the previous paragraphs is suggestive of elements which might be incorporated into a model of mixed ability teaching – an ideal set of circumstances for its most effective operation. These include a style of school and departmental management which can find means of introducing it appropriate to the school context, adequate support in the school's locality, a teaching staff with certain characteristics in terms of previous experience, their perceptions of the nature of their particular subject disciplines and of their role in the classroom, and a school organization capable of responding to whatever requirements become apparent – changes in timetabling, the deployment of staff, the use of buildings or the production and management of resources. It is, of course, extremely unlikely that any school will find its situation completely favourable in all aspects to the introduction of this, or probably any other, innovation. The extent to which the circumstances which we have found to facilitate or constrain teachers working with mixing ability groups are present, however, may provide schools and departments with guidelines concerning the advisibility of attempting to move towards mixed ability grouping and also the kinds of areas which may require special attention should they decide to do so.

We have been concerned in this report to establish why schools 'go mixed ability' and to document teachers' views of the pros and cons of this method of organization. Its major advantages may be summarized as follows: it gives pupils a fresh start and avoids labelling pupils at an early age; closely related to this, it keeps opportunities open for all pupils for a longer period; it avoids other disadvantages associated particularly with streaming such as the creation of disaffected sink groups and injustices arising from difficulties in allocating pupils to streams; and lastly, it creates a school and classroom community which favours certain aspects of personal and social development, is conducive to improved behaviour among pupils and greater work satisfaction among teachers. To be set against these are the major disadvantages reported by teachers of lowered attainment among more able pupils, difficulties experienced by the less able and the increased burden on teachers in terms of producing or locating suitable resources.

These advantages and disadvantages have been frequently stated in recent years and are now part of the well-rehearsed arguments for and against mixed ability teaching; because of this there is a danger that they fail to receive the continued scrutiny on a school-to-school and indeed classroom-to-classroom basis which they demand. In Chapter Two, for example, we presented a series of questions concerning the concept of the 'fresh start'. This sounds a laudable idea and when put into practice may indeed have positive outcomes. There is a possibility however that those who advocate mixed grouping in order to enable pupils to begin with a clean slate may simply be disguising poor liaison with primary schools, and taking insufficient account of the very real differences which exist in the interests and abilities of 11-year-old children. Unless such differences are recognized and catered for by an appropriate teaching method, the fresh start might well prove somewhat stale for pupils at the extremes of the ability range. The concept of 'labelling' also merits attention; we have noted how readily the tripartite division of pupils into the able, average and less able dominated our discussions with teachers on mixed ability teaching. When and how are such diagnoses made? Given all that is known on teacher expectation, how far is mixed ability teaching really an improvement on the 'institutionalized' labelling of schools which group their pupils on the basis of ability?

And the social advantages which form a major part of the justification for mixed ability grouping – how far are these really achieved? In the first phase of the Banbury project which we referred to in the first chapter of this report it was found that among 11- to 13-year-olds in mixed ability classes friendship choices were less often limited to pupils of similar social class and academic ability and that less able children particularly were more content with their form placement in the mixed ability system as compared with those in streamed groups (Newbold, 1977). In the later stage of the enquiry, when the pupils were studied again in their fourth year, it was found that friendship patterns at this stage were little affected by the grouping system through which pupils had come although the authors comment that 'Those who look to mixed ability groups to provide greater social homogeneity in schools can take some comfort from the fact that in strong friendships, greater mixing by VRQ and socio-economic group does exist among pupils whose early grouping background was a mixed ability one' (Postlethwaite and Denton, 1978). It was also found that pupils from a mixed ability background had better attitudes towards the school as a social community at the end of the fifth year although attitudes to school as a working community seemed not to be significantly affected by early grouping differences. These and our own findings point to a need for teachers to examine more closely the nature of the advantages, loosely labelled 'social', which are so frequently claimed for mixed ability teaching. We found a marked tendency for such advantages to be assumed as the inevitable correlate of heterogeneous ability groups, in much the same way as in the early years of comprehensive reorganization it was assumed that the mere juxtaposition of pupils of different abilities under one roof would lead to increased social cohesiveness. Studies, however, have indicated that this was not necessarily so (Kawwa and Robertson, 1970; Reid, 1970 and 1972).

The perceived disadvantages of mixed ability grouping merit similar probing. Many teachers, for example, reported difficulties in catering for the extremes of the ability range, but most had great difficulty in identifying what it was that the able or less able child was not achieving in a mixed ability class that he would have achieved in a class with a more restricted range of ability. Here again, the Banbury findings are pertinent. Among the 11- to 13-year-olds the relative effects of different grouping systems on academic progress appeared small compared with other factors. No evidence of under-achievement on the part of high VRQ pupils was found, and there did seem some support for the view that lower ability pupils achieved higher standards when taught in mixed ability groups. At the end of the fifth year, there was some evidence of better overall performance in public examinations by less able pupils whose early secondary experience had been in the mixed ability situation without any lowering of overall levels of attainment achieved by the more able. The researchers found few significant differences between the systems in the levels of attainment achieved on individual subjects.

It should be emphasized that these results do not conflict with our own findings. The Banbury enquiry was concerned only with the effects of first-year mixed ability teaching and, as is apparent from the evidence cited in Chapter Six, many teachers found few difficulties at this stage. To raise questions concerning the advantages and disadvantages which our teachers identified is not to cast doubt on the value of their evidence, and we repeat here our conviction that research has too often ignored the most obvious and arguably one of the most sound forms of data – that derived from detailed discussion with those who, day by day, are able to experience what happens at what used to be called the chalk-face. As we noted in Chapter Two, we were extremely fortunate in this study to find a sample of teachers with a wide range of backgrounds and experiences working in a variety of mixed ability settings. Our intention in posing questions such as those above is to draw attention to the need for continual monitoring by schools and teachers of their collective and individual thinking particularly in relation to aims and outcomes and to test such thinking against any evidence which can be gathered relating to what really happens for children in the school and classroom. There are now many pleas and in some instances, demands, being made for such self-examination in many parts of the education service. Grouping practices at secondary level particularly merit such scrutiny by individual schools for there are no certain outcomes, either positive or negative, which can be assumed to follow inevitably from mixed ability grouping or, probably, from any other form of organization. What is achieved or not achieved for the pupil, in academic, social and personal terms, will depend on a complex array of circumstances, and it has been our task in this report to attempt to shed some light on these.

Appendix A

Tables and Figures referred to in the Text

(NOTE: The first figure in the table number in all cases indicates the chapter to which the table refers, e.g. Table 4.1A is the first table in the Appendix to which reference is made in Chapter 4)

Table 2.1A: *Subject Classification*

Main subject classification	Subjects included within main subject classification
1. Aesthetic subjects	Art, craft, design, graphics, photography, pottery, printing, sculpture.
2. Commerce	Office practice, shorthand, typing.
3. Domestic Studies	Child care, cookery, domestic science, dress, health education, home economics, home management, money management, needlework, nutrition.
4. English	Drama, English (except when taught as part of an integrated course), film studies, library studies, literature, speech, TV studies.

158

5. Integrated Humanities (with English)	English, geography, history, religious education. Also called: Interdisciplinary Enquiry (IE, IDE), civics, environmental studies (not science based) general studies (not remedial), humanities, social studies.
6. Integrated Humanities (without English)	Geography, history and religious education. Also called: Interdisciplinary Enquiry (IE, IDE), civics, environmental studies (not science based), general studies (not remedial), humanities, social studies.
7. Non-integrated Humanities	Careers counselling, current affairs, economics, geography, geology, history, moral education, personal development, religious education, sex education, social education, sociology.
8. Modern Languages	French, German, Greek, Italian, Latin, Punjabi, Russian, Spanish, Urdu, European studies.
9. Mathematics	Computer studies, mathematics, statistics.
10. Music	Music.
11. Physical Education	Athletics, dance, games, gymnastics, physical education, swimming.
12. Remedial Education	Remedial education, remedial reading. Also called: form subjects, general studies.
13. Integrated Science	Combined science, environmental studies (science based), general science, junior science, Nuffield science, science.
14. Non-integrated Science	Biology, chemistry, electronics, human biology, physics, project technology, rural science.
15. Technical Studies	Boys' craft, car maintenance, engineering drawing, heavy cr' ft, metalwork, technical drawing, .echnical studies, woodwork.

Figure 2.1A: *The distribution of teachers in the sample by length of teaching experience (N = 479)*

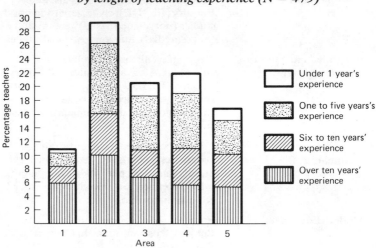

Figure 2.2A: *The previous teaching experience of staff in sample (N = 463)[1]*

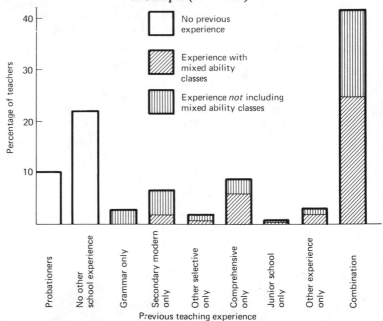

[1] Information on previous experience was not available for 16 teachers.

Table 5.1A: *Problems raised within departments*

Nature of problems	Percentage Heads of Department responding*†
Problems associated with remedial children or children of low academic attainment.	25
Problems associated with the shortage of resources and the selection and preparation of material.	25
Control and discipline problems	15
Problems associated with attempts to teach class as a whole.	13
Problems concerned with meeting needs of able pupils.	10
Problems associated with teaching (unspecified) unfamiliar levels of ability.	5

*(The same Head of Department may be included in more than one category.)
†105 of the 169 Heads of Department interviewed contributed items.

Table 5.2A: *Areas of research suggested by teachers*

Areas of research	Percentage of items (N = 464)
Classroom method and organization	19
Outcomes of mixed ability teaching	15
Institutional factors affecting mixed ability teaching	13
The more able pupil	10
The less able pupil	9
Resources	7
Assessment	6
Staff and pupil attitudes	5
Initial and in-service training	5
Aims and objectives	4
Other	7

Number of teachers contributing items = 332

Table 5.3A: *The citing of disadvantages for the more able pupil in mixed ability classes and teachers' perceptions of the suitability of their subject for teaching to mixed ability groups*

Subject suitability for mixed ability work	Concern for able pupils	
	Declared %	Not declared %
Subject suitable	35	59
Subject unsuitable or suitable only in some respects	65	41
Total number of teachers*	236	157

$x^2 = 22.95$ $p < .001$
*(Ten teachers with no main subject are omitted from this table.)

Appendix B

Catering for Pupils with Special Needs (see Chapter Four)

Arrangements made by Schools for Pupils with Special Needs

Example 1 demonstrates a variety of provision for different areas of disadvantage. An 11–16 school with approximately 1,100 pupils representing the range of ability in its locality, it offered its main support to less able pupils through the faculty structure, with each faculty having a member of staff who taught a remedial group. The remedial classes for various subjects in the first three years may be summarized as follows:

Year Group	Percentage of Pupils Withdrawn				N
	English	Maths	Science	Social Science	
	%	%	%	%	
Year 1	14	13	7	5	231
Year 2	14	9	—	—	208
Year 3	19	8	7	8	190

Pupils were initially identified for these classes on the basis of primary records and in particular reading age, with consultation between the remedial specialist and the teachers in the various faculties. The system was designed to prevent children being isolated for all subjects in one static remedial group, although there was a tendency for a core of the same pupils to appear in the remedial classes in different subjects. Whilst special tuition on a departmental basis provided the crux of the school's provision for the less able, other support systems existed. Around ten per cent of first-year children were extracted individually from English twice a week to attend a handwriting and spelling clinic. Fourteen children, comprising a vertical group drawn from different age ranges, attended a special 'haven' each morning. These were children displaying a combination of educational and 'emotional behavioural' problems, and the haven was designed to provide a secure base where the curriculum was designed to 'take the sting out of education', through activities such as drama, art, visits to places of interest, etc. In the afternoons pupils from the haven attended classes in English and mathematics. Over half of the pupils in the refuge group came from the fifth

163

year, reflecting the higher incidence of special difficulties in this age group. Fourth- and fifth-year pupils with academic weakness in the various curricular areas were catered for by the provision of non-examination classes.

The school was exceptional, in making provision for other potentially disadvantaged children – the most able. Teachers were asked to identify particularly gifted children and these were allocated a tutor according to the particular nature of their giftedness. Whilst such children were not extracted from normal groups as were their less gifted counterparts, tutors were expected to devise ways of providing additional stimulation for them through extra-curricular activity, which sometimes took the simple form of coffee parties where there was an opportunity to experience discussion of a kind not often possible in a mixed ability class.

Example 2   In contrast to the school described in the preceding paragraphs, the school in Example 2 sought to cater for the needs of the less able through a separate remedial class. This policy was based largely on the previous experience of the head that children with learning difficulties tended to be overlooked if taught in classes with other children. Such children frequently had difficulties in relating to a large group of their peers and liked to attach themselves to a father or mother figure. Unless provision was made for them in a separate academic/social unit they tended to 'drift around the school' and lost out academically *because* they lost out socially. Children were identified for the remedial class principally on the basis of a reading age score obtained from their primary schools. The school, which had 996 pupils representing a wide range of ability, had placed 18 per cent of the less able pupils in two remedial classes in the first year, 16 per cent in the second year, seven per cent in the third year, and eight per cent in the fourth. There were no remedial pupils in the fifth year as it was the last year with a grammar school intake. In addition to separate remedial provision in the first four years, a few (approximately four per cent) children were withdrawn from five periods of French in the first and second years for extra tuition in mathematics and English. After entry a child might be allocated to a remedial class or recommended for withdrawal at a regular meeting of all staff teaching his particular year-group. Such a pupil might be transferred back to the mainstream after discussion between the head of the remedial department, the school counsellor and the director of studies, but although numbers in separate remedial classes diminished up the school, there was nonetheless the problem of a number of children who never rejoined their abler counterparts.

It was considered important that the teachers of the less able did not suffer by association; the head of the remedial department received the same scale of post as the head of English, and his upper school counterpart, the head of non-examination studies was salaried at Scale III level.

Example 3   The third example, a small developing school with only years 1–3 and 411 pupils at the time of the enquiry, focused its help for the less able on reading skills. Ten per cent of first year pupils, identified from primary records as having a reading age two or more years behind their chronological age, were taught in a separate remedial class where the central activity was described as a 'crash course' in reading. After the first year pupils were integrated into ordinary classes, a process which was described as having 'obvious problems'; however, it was felt that integration had to take place some day, and the concentration on basic reading skills 'at least saved them from illiteracy'. Reinforcement was provided in the second and third years, when the pupils were withdrawn from French to return to their remedial teacher for extra reading.

Example 4 is of a city school with around 1,500 pupils and a balanced comprehensive intake which at the time of the enquiry was moving from a system of having separate remedial classes to one of withdrawal. Less able children in the second and third years – around eight per cent of each year group – were still taught in remedial groups, but first-year pupils with difficulties were now withdrawn from various lessons in accordance with their particular difficulties. The decision to change to withdrawal had been prompted by two major considerations; first it had been found that some pupils in previous remedial classes requiring special help in reading and writing were nevertheless quite good at numerical skills and second, it had proved extremely difficult to integrate children into ordinary classes once they had been in the remedial group. There had also been some disquiet at the old procedure of allocating children to remedial groups at the outset of their secondary education on the basis of primary records and reading scores. Under the new system all children were placed in mixed ability groups for the early weeks of their secondary school careers and were tested on reading skills, their scores being compared with their primary records. Children were then selected for withdrawal from particular subjects and in some cases, a child might be withdrawn for as much as 80 per cent of the timetable. Around 17 per cent of first-year children were withdrawn for some part of the time, and the policy was to reintegrate them to ordinary teaching groups gradually, subject by subject, avoiding sudden total reintegration. As integration was the aim, the emphasis was not only on basic skills but also on providing a curriculum, similar in content to that followed by other children, and this was the task of three remedial teachers who had to cope with 45 first year withdrawals and 15 and 22 children in the second- and third-year remedial classes. Reintegration proved most difficult in modern languages, where the chances of catching up missed work were few. All the present first-year children who were withdrawn spent some time learning French but this policy was under review. A small percentage of fourth- and fifth-year pupils (around five per cent) were withdrawn for further tuition in basic skills. These were children who for their first three years had been taught in a separate remedial class.

Example 5 resembles the previous example in its adoption of a policy of withdrawal and of a 'diagnostic' period. It had however a markedly different kind of catchment, drawing its pupils from a rural mining community with very few children coming from parents in professional or managerial occupations. For each new intake a list of children likely to require special help was drawn up on the basis of information contained in the common profile form submitted by all the feeder primaries and also from discussions between the first year tutors and the heads of the primary schools. The profile form, which was amongst the most detailed primary record encountered is reproduced on pages 168–71. In the first few weeks all children were taught together in mixed ability groups and the two remedial staff went into lessons in maths and English to watch out for children with difficulties and especially to observe those already listed, and to give help as required. Staff meetings were then held and a decision made concerning which children should be withdrawn. Unlike Example 4, pupils were withdrawn from English and mathematics only; in the former case withdrawal was for three periods a week, whilst in mathematics, it was for all five periods. Seventeen per cent of children attended these withdrawal groups in the first year and this declined to 13 and nine per cent in the second and third years. Withdrawal persisted in the fourth and fifth years where around five per cent of pupils were receiving special help. The advantages of withdrawal over segregation were seen as being that the less able were not deprived of access to 'all the exciting areas'. It was, however, in the head's view, questionable how much benefit they derived from these as they 'haven't got the skills to draw on many experiences'. In terms of their academic progress, segregation might be an effective strategy but the social benefits of integration would be lost: 'Social integration is more important than academic achievement for the least able.'

Example 6   is of a city school with 1,000 pupils, which had one designated remedial class in each of the first three year groups, combined with a system of withdrawals. The remedial groups consisted of around twenty children (ten per cent of each year group) and a major reason for teaching them as a separate group was given as 'child security' – providing a support which for many was lacking at home. All children were screened for reading difficulties on entry and the English department 'nominated' pupils for allocation to the remedial class and for withdrawal. At the time of the enquiry 14 per cent of first-year children and 19 per cent of second-year pupils were withdrawn; there were no withdrawals from the third year on, but this was unusual; in previous years older children had been withdrawn for special help. In contrast to the school described in Example 5, pupils were withdrawn (in most cases for tuition in reading) from *games, home economics* and *craft.*

Example 7   has been selected because it demonstrates procedures for distinguishing among children with different *levels* of reading difficulty and treating groups differently. This school had changed some five years previously from having separate remedial classes to a system of withdrawal and claimed that an improvement in the attitudes of the less able became apparent. Pupils on entry were given a group reading test and those identified as having reading ages of 9.8 years or less took the Standard Reading Tests (Daniels, J. C. and Diack, H., 1972). These tests aim to provide diagnostic information concerning a number of sub-skills related to reading and also provide norms and/or achievement ages to indicate children's level of performance. The school's aim in giving these further tests was to identify children with reading ages of 9.5 years or less. Those with reading ages of nine years or below went each day to the school's 'extra-teaching centre' for half an hour's special tuition in reading skills. Those with reading ages between 9 and 9.5 years attended the centre every other day.

The head described the school as having a 'broad mix of ability, slightly skewed to above average' and the incidence of deprivation in the catchment area he assessed as very low. Only five per cent of pupils in each of the first four years were diagnosed as requiring extra teaching, falling to two per cent in the fifth year. The mathematics department operated its own extraction programme and it was the intention that eventually each faculty should have someone with a particular interest in the needs of the less able who would give help as required to the remedial specialists in the extra teaching centre and that the remedial specialists might also develop a peripatetic role, advising staff in the faculties. It was also hoped that the extra teaching centre might eventually be extended to provide enrichment programmes for the more able. At the time of the enquiry, faculty heads kept a record of those outstanding in their subjects and there were both junior and senior clubs intended to provide a variety of activities to stretch the able. It was felt, however, that because of their voluntary nature, they were unable to assist as many pupils as they ought and in the head's view were a 'worthy but amateurish' attempt at meeting the problem.

Another school in the enquiry resembled Example 7 in varying arrangements for pupils in accordance with their degree of reading retardation. Children identified as having a reading age below eight years, using the Schonell reading tests, were withdrawn from English and enquiry studies, whilst those with reading ages between eight and nine were withdrawn for half a day for eight weeks for an intensive structured course in reading. Pupils with reading ages of nine years or more were catered for in ordinary mixed ability classes.

Example 8   is of a large inner city school with nearly 2,000 pupils, around forty per cent of whom were drawn from immigrant families. Whilst a wide range of ability was present in the intake, the average reading age was nine months behind chronological age. The catchment area of the school was described by the head as being 'deprived' with a high incidence of single parent families. The school's policy towards children with reading or learning difficulties was one of withdrawal the head believing that 'segregation was simply a form of streaming'. Children with a reading age of eight-and-a-half or less were withdrawn from modern languages for five periods a week for intensive reading tuition; around one-third of children were withdrawn in the first three years and almost half of these were trying to master English as a second language. In the fourth and fifth years, the number of children being withdrawn had decreased to approximately one-sixth of pupils.

The school had four full-time remedial staff, who in addition to teaching reading skills to withdrawal groups, were also timetabled to spend about a quarter of their time with each department. The aim of this was to enable them to work with mainstream groups, to provide an additional resource in classrooms where children with learning difficulties might sometimes be difficult to cater for and to advise their colleagues in the various departments on suitable materials and approaches.

Sixth-form pupils undertaking a social studies course were also deployed in helping teachers with first year classes. Their assistance might include helping the younger children to understand instructions, find equipment and generally organize themselves for the task in hand.

EXAMPLE 5 – PRIMARY PROFILE FORM

CONFIDENTIAL   *PRIMARY PUPIL PROFILE*

TRANSFER FROM......................................   TO ....SCHOOL

SCHOOL   Christian Name: ....

Surname:...   DATE OF BIRTH ....

....   Position in Family ....

Name of Parent or Guardian.. Tel. No ....

Address and Telephone No. where parent/guardian may be contacted during school hours:

....

Previous school(s) attended, with dates of transfer ....

....

....

Father's occupation.......................................   Mother's occupation ....

Where the 5 point scale is used please circle in red the appropriate letters

SECTION A
Child's Interest in Appearance
a. Always very neat and tidy
b. Takes care of appearance within limits
c. Usually tidy
d. Rather careless about appearance
e. Completely disinterested

Parents Interest in Child's Appearance
a. Very High
b. High
c. Acceptable
d. Low
e. Very low

SECTION B   PERSONALITY

1. *INITIATIVE*
a. Very quick to seize opportunities
b. Not afraid to make decisions
c. Can make decisions but prefers guidance
d. Always plays safe
e. Never grasps an opportunity

2. *LEADERSHIP*
a. A natural leader
b. Capable of getting the best from others
c. Not able to persuade others to follow
d. Prefers to follow
e. Too easily influenced by others

3. *RELIABILITY*
a. Thoroughly imaginative and trustworthy
b. Completely trustworthy but imaginative
c. Generally reliable
d. Finds it hard to resist temptation
e. Finds it impossible to resist temptation

4. *SELF-CONFIDENCE*
a. Completely self-assured
b. Usually confident
c. Average mixture of assurance and reticence
d. Shy and reticent
e. Extremely timid

5. *BEHAVIOUR*
a. Exemplary
b. Usually well behaved
c. Occasional noticeable lapses
d. Aggressive
e. Sly and deceitful

6. *SOCIABILITY*
a. Very Popular
b. Generally gets on well with people
c. Acceptable to most of his/her peers
d. Something of a 'lone wolf'
e. Positively avoided

7. *PUNCTUALITY AND ATTENDANCE*
a. Exemplary
b. Genuine absences only
c. Occasionally absent without good reason
d. Frequently late
e. Frequent or prolonged absences

SECTION C

PARENTAL INTEREST
a. Keen to give every support possible
b. Willing to co-operate but will not push themselves
c. Interested only in so far as their child is directly concerned
d. Interested only for the purpose of complaining
e. Totally disinterested

SECTION D

APTITUDES AND INTERESTS
Please specify
(a) *In School*
   (i) Aptitudes and interests e.g. in Art, Crafts, Expression, Music
   (ii) Weaknesses and those activities in which the pupil finds difficulty
(b) *Out of School*
   Special Interests

SECTION E

Please indicate:
   (i) any physical defects or handicaps of pupil
   (ii) any special family etc., circumstances which should be known

Date: Head's signature:...

SPECIAL HELP – PROFILE

Please complete this questionnaire for any child whom you consider may
need extra help, for any reason whatsoever at:
.... SCHOOL.

NAME OF CHILD: ....

1. (a) Does the child hold a pencil correctly? If not, how?
     (b) With which hand
2. Can the child (a) write   (b) print   own name?
3. Can the child copy?
     (a) from print
     (b) from writing
     (c) from blackboard
4. Can the child compose simple sentences?
     (a) on own
     (b) with help

   (c) not at all
5. Does the child
    (a) speak clearly
    (b) wear spectacles
    (c) have a hearing defect
6. Does the child experience difficulties in working from left to right?
7. Can the child attempt free writing?
8. (a) Are the phonic sounds of letters of the alphabet recognized?
    (b) If not, which are not?
9. Can the child differentiate between capital and lower case letters?
10. Can the child recognize and read phonic sounds?
    (a) at the beginning of words
    (b) at the end of words
11. Can the child recognize and read consonant blends?
    (a) at the beginnings of phonically simple words
    (b) at the ends of phonically simple words
12. Please elaborate on any failure in (10) and (11)
13. Can the child recognize polysyllabic phonically simple words?
14. Does the child syllabize words?
15. What other combinations of sounds does the child recognize?
16. Does the child 'reverse' words when writing?
17. What method(s) of reading has (have) been employed?
18. Which reading schemes?
19. Which books have been read by the child recently?
20. Does the child (a) remember?
                   (b) comprehend?
21. What special interests has the child?
22. What problems accompany learning difficulties?
    (a) Behaviour
    (b) Qualities of character
    (c) Habits
23. Can the child
    (a) Recognize?
    (b) Write?
    (c) Repeat?
    (d) Count in sequence, numbers?
24. Can the child add in H.T.U'S?
    If not, with what limitations?
25. Can the child cope with simple subtraction?
    (a) limitations
    (b) method used
26. Does the child know any tables by rote?
27. Can the child attempt multiplication? Division?
    (a) short
    (b) long
    (c) limitations
28. Please state standard reached in
    (a) weight
    (b) length

    (c) capacity
    (d) area
    (e) fractions
    (f) decimals
29. Which coins can be recognized?
30. Up to how much money can the child reckon, using coins?
31. What work has been covered, using money?
32. How accurately can the child tell the time?
33. Please state (a) Texts used by child in the past
              (b) Current text
34. Other relevant information.

References

ADELMAN, C. (1976). 'Mixed ability classes – some typical problems', *Cambridge Journal of Education*, **6**, 1/2.

ASSISTANT MASTERS ASSOCIATION (1974). *Mixed Ability Teaching*. London: AMA.

BAILEY, C. (1976). 'Mixed ability teaching and the defence of subjects', *Cambridge Journal of Education*, **6**, 1/2.

BARKER LUNN, J. C. (1970). *Streaming in the Primary School* Slough: NFER.

BORG, W. R. (1964). *An Evaluation of Ability Grouping*. Utah State University.

BRIAULT, E. AND SMITH, F. (1980a). *Falling Rolls in Secondary Schools*. Slough: NFER.

BRIAULT, E. AND SMITH, F. (1980b). *Falling Rolls in Secondary Schools* (second volume). Slough: NFER.

BRIDGES, D. (1976). 'The social organisation of the classroom and the philosophy of mixed ability teaching', *Cambridge Journal of Education*, **6**, 1/2.

CRONBACH, L. J. (1978). Designing Educational Evaluations. Occasional paper, Stanford Evaluation Consortium, Stanford, California (mimeo).

DAVIES, R. P. (1975). *Mixed Ability Grouping: Possibilities and Experiences in the Secondary School*. London: Temple Smith.

DEPARTMENT OF EDUCATION AND SCIENCE (1971). Education Survey 15: *Slow Learners in Secondary Schools*. London: HMSO.

DEPARTMENT OF EDUCATION AND SCIENCE (1978). *Mixed Ability Work in Comprehensive Schools*. London: HMSO.

DEPARTMENT OF EDUCATION AND SCIENCE (1979). *Aspects of Secondary Education in England: A Survey by HM Inspectors of Schools:* London: HMSO.

DEPARTMENT OF EDUCATION AND SCIENCE (1980). *Report by HM Inspectors on Educational Provision by the Inner London Education Authority*. London: DES.

ELLIOT, J. (Ed) (1976). 'Mixed ability teaching', *Cambridge Journal of Education*, **6**, 1/2.

HINSON, M. (1977). Presidential Address to the Annual Conference of the National Association for Remedial Education.

HOYLE, E. (1969). 'How does the curriculum change?', *Journal of Curriculum Studies*, Nov.

HUGHES, M. G. (1972). The role of the Secondary school head. University of Wales Ph D thesis. University College, Cardiff.

ILEA (1976). *Mixed Ability Grouping*. Report of an ILEA Inspectorate survey. London: ILEA.

References 173

KAWWA, T. AND ROBERTSON, T. S. (1970). 'Mixing and friendship choices.' In: MONKS, T. G. (Ed) *Comprehensive Education in Action.* Slough: NFER.
KELLY, A. V. (1974). *Teaching Mixed Ability Classes.* London: Harper & Row.
KELLY, A. V. (1978). *Mixed Ability Grouping: Theory and Practice.* London: Harper & Row.
MONKS, T. G. (1968). *Comprehensive Education in England & Wales.* Slough: NFER.
MORRISON, C. M. (1976). *Ability Grouping and Mixed Ability Grouping in Secondary Schools.* Scottish Council for Research in Education: Edinburgh.
NEWBOLD, D. (1975). 'Mixed ability or streaming?' In: *The School as a Centre of Enquiry.* Banbury School: Pubansco.
NEWBOLD, D. (1977). *Ability Grouping – The Banbury Enquiry.* Slough: NFER.
OWEN, J. G. (1970). 'Educational Innovation: the human factor', *Journal of Educational Administration and History,* June.
PASSOW, H. A. (1966). 'The maze of research on ability grouping.' In: YATES, A. J. (Ed) *Grouping in Education.* Hamburg: Unesco Institute of Education. London: John Wiley.
POSTLETHWAITE, K. AND DEWTON, C. (1978). *Streams for the Future.* Banbury: Pubansco.
REID, M. I. (1970). 'Voluntary extra-curricular activities.' In: MONKS, T. G. (Ed) *Comprehensive Education in Action.* Slough: NFER.
REID, M. I. (1972). 'Comprehensive integration outside the classroom', *Educational Research,* **14**, 2.
ROBINSON, K. A. (1973). Aims and Objectives in Mixed Ability Learning. Paper delivered at University of Exeter Department of Education.
ROSS, J. M., BUNTON, W. J. EVISON, P. and ROBERTSON, T. S. (1972). *A Critical Appraisal of Comprehensive Education.* Slough: NFER.
SAMPSON, D. AND PUMFREY, P. (1970). 'A study of remedial education in the secondary stage of schooling', *Remedial Education,* **5**, 3.
SCOTT, P. J. (1976). Non-Streamed Teaching: one Association's Approach to the Problems. An address given to the Council of Subject Teaching Associations, 20.11.76.
WRAGG, E. C. (1976). *Teaching Mixed Ability Groups.* Newton Abbot: David & Charles.
YATES, A. J. (Ed) (1966). *Grouping in Education.* Hamburg: Unesco Institute of Education. London: John Wiley.

Index